Partners at Odds

Werner Weidenfeld

Partners at Odds

The Future of Transatlantic Relations—
Options for a New Beginning

| Verlag Bertelsmann**Stiftung**

Bibliographic information published by Die Deutsche Bibliothek

Die Deutsche Bibliothek lists this publication in the
Deutsche Nationalbibliografie; detailed bibliographic information
is available online at http://dnb.ddb.de

© 2006 Verlag Bertelsmann Stiftung, Gütersloh
Editor: Annette Heuser, Brussels
Translation: Celia Bohannon and Marissa Wright for German Language Services,
Seattle, Washington
Production: Sabine Reimann
Cover illustration: Thomas Kunsch, Bielefeld
Typesetting and print: Hans Kock Buch- und Offsetdruck GmbH, Bielefeld
ISBN-10: 3-89204-880-0
ISBN-13: 978-3-89204-880-0

www.bertelsmann-stiftung.de/verlag

Table of Contents

Introduction: The moment of truth

Several years ago, I published an analysis of transatlantic relations. Back then the relationship seemed less fraught with conflict than now. However, basic political and cultural realities pointed toward the widening rift between Europe and the United States. The societies on both sides of the Atlantic were developing and moving in different directions, leading me to choose the title *America and Europe: Is the Break Inevitable?*

The book stirred up intense debate at the time. While many voiced agreement, critics commented that the question of a possible cultural split was too harsh, too pessimistic. When the war in Iraq made the divergence between Washington and a number of European allies truly obvious, my theories were suddenly praised as visionary. Unfortunately, by then the book was out of print.

I took this as an opportunity to further develop my concept and bring it up to date. This in turn has become a new book. Now as then, my goal is to take a reasoned look at the situation—not dazzled by politicians' manipulative dramatizations, but rather focused on the societies' deeper dimensions, their self-images and cultures.

On the surface, a transatlantic campaign of smiles continues to await us—except during severe conflicts. People will smile for the camera. Top politicians will embrace one another. No smile, no handshake will be too much of a strain. People will roll out the warmhearted goodwill. Europeans' sense of self-esteem will take wing. Someone finally knows how to cosset Europe's proud soul. The dramatists on the international scene will rub their hands together with glee.

Behind this polished, glossy facade lies the abyss of transatlantic reality. It is important to face this reality. It isn't essential here that the American president and German chancellor like each other, or that the American president and British prime minister trust each other. Particularly in German-American relations, the chance for a fresh start arises again and again. What will be important is how the societies in America and Europe define themselves. Their representatives, the presidents and heads of state, are simply the messengers, the sounding boards for what is really going on deep down in these societies. Anyone who has a feel for the self-perceptions prevailing on both sides of the Atlantic must be alarmed. Never—since the end of World War II—has the pulse on the two sides of the Atlantic followed a more different rhythm.

One must acknowledge that the common bond of the Cold War was an exceptional situation in transatlantic relations, and for the German-American friendship in particular. From a historical perspective, relations have always been ambivalent—influenced by a wish for nearness and yet mental distance, shaped by admiration and aversion. America, a continent that lives for the future, is admired and disdained by Europe, a continent that lives from its history—and vice versa. American nonchalance at exploring new frontiers stands in direct contrast to Europe's highly complex history of self-criticism. Both approaches have their allure—but they are only marginally compatible.

This fundamental tenet of transatlantic ambivalence was suspended during the era of the Cold War, which brought the souls of America and Europe into complete harmony. The threat from the East to the common ideal of freedom was the rock the Atlantic community was built upon. The concept of the human being as an individual person (West) was pitted against the human being as part of a collective (East). America defended its own ethos in Berlin—and the Germans warmly thanked America for it.

This exceptional situation is long past; even its echoes fade in memory. The societies have returned to their normal tradition of ambivalence; only the lingering sentimentality of transatlantic dialogue has yet to register this new reality. But someday the moment of truth will arrive for the world of politics, and it will no longer be able to conceal social reality in a fog of nostalgia. Then it will have to call a spade a spade. Politicians will have to answer the question of whether and how they can put a stop to transatlantic alienation.

The key to the growing differences between America and Europe lies in their vastly different perceptions of threat and risk. Since September 11, 2001, America has felt threatened to its very core, its

10

security seriously in question for the first time in its history. The principle of deterrence is obsolete. America is living in a nightmare. It is attempting to ensure its own security—and refuses to ask anyone in the world if its measures are justified.

The Europeans are taking quite a different approach, now that they too are lodged squarely in the sights of international terrorism. Even those who ignored the attack in Madrid as an initial wakeup call had to acknowledge by July 2005 with the London bombings that terrorism had finally arrived in Europe and could strike again at any time in any country. Nonetheless, Europeans still entertain fundamental doubts about the legitimacy of American methods of dealing with international terrorism and American military action. They want to use a multilateral approach to contain these conflicts. They want to make peace, not war. Aside from self-defense, they see a U.N. mandate as the only legitimate basis for the use of force.

Samuel Huntington is mistaken when he speaks of a "clash of civilizations." A different set of issues is taking on new urgency. As a consequence, a "battle of risk cultures" is brewing between Europe and America, based mainly on this difference in threat and risk perception on both sides of the Atlantic. This battle has an entirely different political and cultural dimension than the superficial observation of polite interaction between top political leaders. It is about the very core of a society's self-image and identity. So what can the political world do?

Politicians have the following options:

- They can continue to maintain the old sentimental bond. It will wear thinner with each passing year—until it dissolves entirely because it has no basis in reality.
- They can continue to smooth-talk and dismiss the situation as a temporary dissonance in the atmosphere—and gain some time in the hopes of clearer skies on the horizon.
- They can acknowledge the truth and pursue one of two courses: Either the different risk cultures will lead to different strategies that allow selective cooperation at best, or the governments in America and Europe will undertake an enormous effort to craft a common transatlantic risk culture.

One way or another—we will not be able to avoid the moment of truth indefinitely, either in Europe or America. The sooner we start adopting strategic realism, the better. With this book, I hope to further develop the analytical scheme I presented in *America and Europe: Is the Break Inevitable?* and contribute to establishing the necessary clarity.

1 The transatlantic relationship in a new political environment

From the sentiment of friendship to transatlantic sobriety

World politics stands on the verge of a new epoch. Evidence appears almost daily of our entry into an era fraught with risk and disarray. We have known the terrorist attacks of al-Qaida, North Korea's uncertain return to the Treaty on the Non-proliferation of Nuclear Weapons and revival of its nuclear program, Iran's reactivation of the nuclear facility in Isfahan and then of the uranium-enriching plant in Natan. We have seen Palestinian suicide bombings in Israel and retaliatory actions by the Israeli government, instability in Afghanistan and Iraq and an uncertain future for Saudi Arabia following the death of King Fahd. The focus of world politics is zooming in once again on transnational crises and security threats.

It would be naive to expect the German-American friendship and the Euro-American partnership to remain untouched by the upheaval in world politics. Nevertheless, the state of the partnership is clear. The old sentimentality, which kept the partnership superficially intact out of nostalgia, is dead; the emotional warmth has cooled. A new generation has arrived—and with it a new lexicon of partnership. The rhetoric of CARE packages, the Berlin airlift and Hoover lunches no longer tugs us toward the future; such terms are museum pieces that remind us of a time gone by. The new present reverberates with harsh criticism and mutual accusations of undermining the partnership. The American pursuit of hegemony now tends toward a unilateralism previously unknown.

One only needs to look below the surface to realize that the transatlantic relationship has eroded. A variety of factors—shifts in foreign policy strategy, growing indifference, the dissolution of personal networks, the generational changing of the guard, a focus on domestic politics, hazier definitions of geographical entities, surprising leaps in political positions—all mean that Germany, Europe and the United States can no longer rely on the certainties that underpinned transatlantic relations for almost 50 years. Caught up in a swirling global political constellation under the dark star of terrorism, links across the Atlantic need to find new solutions to new challenges.

Although the ice age of Euro-American relations has passed, a certain coolness lingers—and for good reason. The European frustration of not being taken seriously by the United States as an equal partner still lingers. The Europeans did not hesitate after the terrorist acts of September 11, 2001; NATO stood ready for defensive action. But to their astonishment, NATO wasn't even needed. The United States took over the operation against terrorism in Afghanistan almost entirely on its own. The European nations came humbly, one by one and to an extent as petitioners, bringing offers of assistance to the halls of power. There, the superpower accepted this or that offer at its own discretion. Europeans' self-image and pride had felt such slights many times over the years during operations in the Balkans. All of this certainly does not secure the foundation for a cordial friendship.

The United States was shaken to its very core on September 11. Even the last remaining superpower can no longer guarantee the safety of its citizens. This is a totally new horizon for a country that throughout its history largely considered itself unassailable. Challenges to American security policy traditionally lay outside the country's own borders. Wherever the American dream of freedom seemed threatened, the United States' ethos was called upon—in divided Germany, in Berlin, in Vietnam, in Somalia, in Yugoslavia and elsewhere. The first threat to the nation's own territory was therefore a traumatic experience.

From the U.S. perspective, it needs more from Europe in the war on terror than the sentiment of friendship. It needs solid performance. But this has mercilessly revealed Europe's military weaknesses, brought on by years of neglecting to modernize its military and arming its forces for outdated battle scenarios.

From the European perspective, however, the European Union's common foreign and security policy (CFSP) ranks as a success story. Since 1970, Europe had sought to clear the hurdle of the final prerogative of national sovereignty—that each nation establishes its own foreign and security policy. The EU's coordination networks have steadily grown denser, their instruments more precise. But to this day the

CFSP relies upon building a consensus based on collective will. Even now that the European Union is on the verge of having collective crisis intervention troops ready for rapid deployment, direct, military intervention in bloody international conflict is very difficult to imagine.

What to European minds, against the backdrop of European history, counts as a historic step forward seems fairly irrelevant to the more action-oriented Americans. Europe's weakness downright provokes the United States' singular strength.

What good to the United States is a European partner whose hands are tied when it really matters? In troubled times, the United States thinks along the traditional lines of its own interests. Europe, in its self-induced weakness, comes to mind as an afterthought—most likely when reconstruction is on the agenda. At the same time, Europeans have stopped deferentially laying their hopes for security, freedom and peace on the strong shoulders of the Atlantic world power.

A time of transatlantic sobriety has begun. That is not necessarily a bad thing, because it also keeps disappointment in check. But what does this cultural change mean for the cement holding the transatlantic alliance together? Will it crumble? Will it gain renewed substance and strength?

Redefining transatlantic interests

One thing is certain. Since September 11, Europe and America have redefined their interests. In the future, therefore, a positive rationale for the Euro-American partnership will have to be found. The unique success story shared over the last 50 years will continue to influence transatlantic relations for some time. But the old loyalties will not suffice as political and analytical coordinates for the next phase of Euro-American cooperation.

An amicable realignment of transatlantic relations, with gains for both sides, would be very welcome. But the opposite is also possible. In matters of foreign policy, the centrifugal force of international crises and reactions could tug the partners apart. In economic affairs, they could fall victim to unchecked turbulence in transatlantic trade. The two societies could slowly drift in different directions until each fades from the other's view. This scenario could easily lead to a rivalry that would set the tone for transatlantic relations for a long time to come.

But this negative outcome would mean more for Europe and the United States than just a somewhat difficult restructuring of foreign policy priorities. It would rattle the very foundations of European and American identity.

Historically speaking, each partner has always formed part and parcel of the other's identity. The Americans' commitment to rebuilding Europe after World War II has been a key component of the European collective consciousness—especially for Germany. And the European contribution to the evolution of the United States is a leitmotif running through the American psyche that transcends any demographic or ethnic changes.

Thus, for both sides, the loss of their transatlantic partner would do more than just inflict damage in the foreign policy arena. It would lead to a cultural split with disastrous consequences. If we want the partnership to succeed, we must redefine transatlantic relations in a way that not only presents both partners with a common agenda for mutual gain, but also enables each to redefine its own identity while still including the other side.

Rivalries and asymmetries

That the United States and the European Union are important partners for each other is not even in question. The basic objectives of their security, economic, trade and monetary policies and their fundamental perspectives are more or less in agreement. But the actual, concrete interests derived from these roots are not necessarily aligned.

Here the scene is ruled by rivalries and asymmetries, giving rise to the dialectics of transatlantic interconnectedness and rivalry in the economic arena. In matters of security policy, the United States subordinates European resources to its own interests. At the same time, independent European attempts at organization are immediately met with a reflex reaction of mistrust and suspicion. The United States' multilateral thinking extends only to the limits of its own defined interests. Beyond that, unilateralism rules the day.

The following examples characterize the imbalances in the transatlantic relationship:

- As the only credible source of world order since the collapse of the Soviet Union, the United States has repeatedly sought to prove itself the leading nation in global security policy—despite indecision and inefficacy in Haiti and Somalia and in stoking the conflict between China and Taiwan. The attacks of September 11 have propelled this development a giant step forward, as evidenced by the interventions in Afghanistan and Iraq. By comparison, Europe's contribution has fallen far short of initial expectations, as became clear in the Balkans and the war in Kosovo in particular.

- The political personas on either side of the Atlantic have taken different forms. While Americans take it for granted that the United States should set an example for the rest of the world, Europe has not yet brought itself to make that claim.

These asymmetries would be much more significant if they were not tempered considerably by deeply shared values and common structures, as well as by a long tradition of continuity in Euro-American cooperation. Despite occasional periods of turbulence, there has been continuity in the security structure; continuity in constructive conflict resolution with each other; continuity in collaboration around the world, within the United Nations and the OSCE and in acute crisis situations—not to mention continuity with regard to close economic and cultural cooperation.

It cannot be denied that a lack of military strength has relegated Europeans to the role of spectators to this day, as they painfully experienced in the Balkans and to an extent in Afghanistan and Iraq.

However, the relationship between the United States and Europe has never been easy to describe. Relations over the last few decades have featured an odd contradiction: Beneath regular, sometimes spectacular turbulence on the surface, there lay a steady undercurrent of transatlantic friendship that dependably shaped public opinion and the attitudes of society as a whole.

Thus, for example, opinion polls in Germany and the United States showed for decades that Germans and Americans regularly ranked each other's country first in their list of favored nations.[1] The deep feelings of solidarity with the United States during the terrifying

1 For example, see the studies of the German Marshall Fund of the United States (in cooperation with the Chicago Council on Foreign Relations): "Worldviews 2002: European Public Opinion & Foreign Policy" and "American Public Opinion & Foreign Policy." Washington, D. C., and Chicago 2002.

moments of September 11 revealed the common foundation of friendship in a wholly new way. However, cracks in the surface soon reappeared, which the Europeans attributed to growing U.S. unilateralism and its rejection of multilateral negotiation forums in a number of different policy areas, including environmental, economic and security policy.

Then the war in Iraq caused a significant drop in mutual liking and support. Even though friendship ratings since 2003 have risen again and are approaching previous levels, the public in both countries views the relationship coolly. A survey conducted in May and June of 2005 in nine EU countries, Turkey and the United States revealed that all of George W. Bush's efforts to improve relations between Europe and the United States have been in vain: Both Europeans and Americans feel that the relationship remains in poor condition (52 percent of Europeans, 50 percent of Americans). Furthermore, 55 percent of Europeans would like to see more independence from the United States with regard to foreign and security policy. By contrast, the desire for Europe to take on a greater role is growing in the United States: In 2005, 47 percent of Americans were in favor of the European Union becoming a superpower (2004: 41 percent). Although attitudes toward the United States have not improved, fears of growing anti-American resentment have proven unfounded. Despite the fact that 72 percent of Europeans disapprove of President Bush's foreign policy, only 59 percent of them reject a global leadership role for the United States.[2]

Aside from the Iraq effect and the generally positive attitude that existed beforehand, concerns about the future of the partnership have always been a staple of the transatlantic dialogue. The European public regularly speculates about whether the United States has any real interest at all in Europe and whether difficult domestic issues will require the Americans to scale back their international engagement. On the other side of the Atlantic, the question keeps resurfacing of whether Europe—which owes much of its greatness to generous American support after the catastrophe of World War II—even needs the United States anymore.

2   For this data, see: German Marshall Fund of the United States and the Compagnia di San Paolo. "Transatlantic Trends 2005," Washington D.C., www.transatlantic-trends.org/. Survey findings from the Pew Research Center from Summer 2002 and May 2003 confirm this trend.

In contrast to some intellectual dramatizations, the political rhetoric of the post–Cold War period often exaggerated the harmonious accord, as if conflicts of interest, differing opinions, disagreements and frustrations should never occur in friendly relations. On closer scrutiny, both approaches—dramatization of differences, overemphasis on harmony—proved equally unrealistic. Judgments about the current status and future prospects of European-American relations have been thrown somewhat off balance, particularly by the events of September 11 and the war in Iraq. People on both sides of the Atlantic need to regain a sense of proportion.

Paradoxes in the transatlantic relationship

This tension between harmonization and dramatization in the transatlantic relationship is reflected in a number of paradoxes that resurface time and again in several now classic variants:
- NATO links the Europeans and Americans in a security alliance— and yet for any number of reasons, each partner regularly voices doubts about the dependability of the other's security policy. At the same time, different sides postulate the end of NATO as we know it, since the whole reason for its existence has disappeared with the fall of their common enemy, the Soviet Union. Furthermore, February 2003 brought NATO face to face with its toughest crisis ever when Turkey requested a defense plan in case of a war in Iraq. While seeming fairly insignificant at first, this problem nonetheless exposed a break with NATO's procedural principles. NATO abandoned the principle of unanimity for the first time, and—by sidestepping France and persuading Germany and Belgium—arrived at a decision that allowed some members to go ahead with establishing a "coalition of the willing and able." The February crisis was NATO's wake-up call for long-overdue reform to ensure its continued existence.
- The economies of Europe and the United States are closely interwoven in networks of investments and trade—yet the two partners constantly accuse one another of violating the international rules of free trade and pursuing their own advantage at the expense of the other.
- On many occasions, the Europeans have called on the United States to demonstrate leadership. And yet as soon as the United

States starts to take the helm, you can be sure that large segments of the European population will voice significant concern. Conversely, since German unification, the United States has ascribed to the new Germany a natural and necessary leadership role within Europe. But at the same time, a certain sector of American public opinion is wary of this larger and more powerful Germany.

– Time and again, the United States called on the Europeans to finally move ahead decisively with integration and eastern enlargement. Yet as soon as this process began to gain traction, critics in the United States leaped to identify this development as a signal that Europe was turning away from its transatlantic partner.

How to fit all this together? How to reconcile this medley of misunderstanding, sympathetic affection and harsh criticism? How to explain this paradoxical mixture of nearness and distance between Americans and Europeans? The answer will not be found by reviewing the headlines on Euro-American relations from recent years. Burden sharing, protectionism, the nuclear arms debate, trade sanctions, the creation of the International Criminal Court, the Kyoto Protocol, Bush fire, war for cheap oil, abuses at the Guantanamo and Abu Ghraib prisons—catchwords like these symbolize the narrowing of perspectives to focus on specific crisis points, and thus on the mere surface of the relationship. What is called for, however, is an exploration of its multifaceted depths.

The future of the Western world and Euro-American relations will not be decided by any one detail, any single decision about a certain military action, or even any conflict over a specific economic disagreement. Far more crucial to the West will be the question of how to preserve the political and cultural ties at the heart of the relationship between the United States and Europe and keep them vital for the next generation even under changing external conditions. This question has engendered a completely new need for clarity.

Coherent policy between the United States and Europe is therefore neither a matter of course nor a prerequisite for the partnership. Rather, a sufficient level of harmony will be the result of a steady, joint effort.

Any attempt to determine the future role of the transatlantic alliance must first take into account the radical changes in the global political scene since the time of the partnership's inception. Many of the figures and constellations that once played deciding roles in global politics have lost significance in recent years. They no longer have the power to shape strategies for the future and train a new pool of transatlantic leadership. Five changes in international politics have been particularly relevant in this regard:

1. International terrorism has replaced the East-West conflict as the main strategic determinant of international politics and thereby also diminished the overarching significance of traditional security policy. At the same time, the number of actors in the international political arena is growing, together with the scope for cooperation and conflict. A consequence of this development is the relativization of former power structures. The advancement of international law and the globalization of media, with worldwide on-the-spot reporting, contribute to this phenomenon. Although the United States is the only remaining superpower, it has greater difficulty bringing its weight to bear, because military and political pre-eminence are less crucial to resolving today's conflict situations (terrorism, civil war, nuclear proliferation, economic crises).

2. Media globalization has also spawned the densest network of global political connections the world has ever seen. This amplifies the significance of regional conflicts and fundamentalist movements alike. The worldwide network of information and mass media has led to new forms of international conflict. Images of the September 11 attacks have contributed to this as much as real-time market data from Wall Street. Thus, the world of subjective dispositions of people with their desires, hopes and fears is transformed into a world of images and information, a much-courted nerve center of today's societies that captures and holds the attention of the political scene.

3. The traditional concept of national sovereignty is increasingly proving to be a utopian and naive relic of yesteryear. The vast majority of the issues and tasks facing politicians today have long since spilled over national borders. However, the internationalized structure of these problems is not yet matched by any adequate

21

political decision-making structures. As a result, the decision-making capacity of politicians will continue to trickle away—unless they manage to rechannel it in the form of effective international organizations.

4. It is equally important in both Western and Eastern Europe—albeit on different levels—to find a response to the pressure to modernize. Regionalization is a key concept in this issue. Western Europe reacted by implementing the Economic and Monetary Union and introducing a common currency. Concurrent efforts in other political fields are moving toward integration aimed at political union. In Eastern Europe, three topics loom in the foreground of modernization pressures: Differentiation, opening and pluralization. The entry of 10 central and eastern European states into the European Union hinged on reaching a certain level of economic competitiveness. Romania and Bulgaria are expected to follow in 2007, while accession talks with Turkey began in October 2005.

5. A shift of emphasis is underway in Euro-American relations. The trimming of American forces in Europe has diminished the defense and security policy dimension of the relationship, while economic and cultural dimensions loom larger. This has brought a finer balance of economic and political weight between the two continents. The Americans are rediscovering their respect for the old world's dynamic drive.

In its own best interests, America will want to have a presence in what may be the strongest and most vital segment of the world market. Even the Europe of the Fifteen accounted for one-fifth of global imports and exports, though it held only about six percent of the world's population. One-third of the world's currency reserves are found in the European Community. The European Union is one of the biggest trade partners in the world. With the enlargement of the European Union to 25 nations, this potential has grown even further, thus making Europe even more economically indispensable for the United States.

All in all, it must be said that the world political agenda has never embraced as broad a range of topics as now, nor have so many changes occurred simultaneously in so many regions of the world. As the last remaining superpower, the United States had to discover that it could not resolve the plethora of conflicts and threats in the world all on its own. And it recognized that Europe is an irreplaceable partner in overcoming global challenges, such as in the negotiations with Iran on halting uranium enrichment there. These changes mean that both sides must take a long, critical look at the reliability and solidarity of traditional structures. The crucial underpinnings for the future architecture of transatlantic structures will remain contingent upon the political will of the policy-makers involved.

Against this complex backdrop, this book will investigate the conditions and perspectives for a new orientation in transatlantic relations.

After an excursion into the history of transatlantic relations, it will examine the development of the United States following the end of the Cold War and the course of European integration after World War II. Proceeding from this background information, the book will describe how the transatlantic community can find new footing in view of changes in world politics and new global challenges. It will conclude with an evaluation of the partners' prospects. This interpretation aims to elucidate the state of affairs on both sides and offer recommendations for political action.

2 The common elements— a historically developed partnership

The history of the Euro-American partnership goes back to the early years of the United States. Ever since settlers first arrived in North America and the United States was founded, there have been links between Europe and America. This chapter describes the development of relations between the United States and Europe in the 19th century, the debut of America on the European political stage at the start of the 20th century, the relationship in the interwar period, and the construction of the transatlantic community and its most important phases after World War II.

The early days of the transatlantic community

Europe and America—common roots

The United States evolved from the world of ideas embodied in the European enlightenment: reason, human rights, freedom, equality and democracy. The progressive idealism of the European Enlightenment is the source of the American dream and manifest destiny.

For many Europeans, emigration to America represented an act of liberation from the oppressive constraints of Europe. In the creation of the United States of America, a new world was formed.

In this better world, a wealth of ideas from the old continent would be realized more rapidly and more directly than was possible in a Europe frequently caught in the throes of bloody conflicts. In America, the brilliance and continuity of progressive idealism developed in an atmosphere free from the European tendency to lapse into the ambivalence of dogmas and totalitarianism.

In addition to this contribution of European ideas to the founding of the New World, there were also other forms of interchange that are frequently overlooked. Even the foundations of the American social structure—its legal and administrative systems, its religion and customs—were brought from Europe. This meant that Americans would always view Europe as the continent of their roots, the underpinning of their own identity.

Conversely America also has played an important role in the development of European ideas and politics since gaining its independence from Great Britain.[3] Goethe wrote a well-known poem in which he congratulated the Americans on escaping the sad heritage of Europe's feudal structures. Of much greater political significance for European conditions was the prediction made by de Tocqueville in 1835 "that we, like the Americans, will sooner or later achieve almost complete equality."[4]

In other words, from a very early stage, America represented an ideal for the political classes in Europe. After the failed revolution of 1848, countless German democrats who had been particularly inspired by the example of America emigrated to the United States, where they were able to live out their ideas.

In the 19th century, it was above all the ambitious middle classes and democrats in Europe who regarded America as the home of modernity, a country in which origins and class differences were no longer relevant and every citizen could achieve economic and social success based solely on the grounds of ability and performance. And as early as the 1800s, there were Europeans calling for U.S. intervention to support democratic movements in Europe.

Even over and above political idealism, from the outset many Europeans were fascinated by the extraordinary dynamism of American society and the way it transcended the narrow geographical and social constraints of Europe. The idea of the self-made man, the mobility of American society and the relative ease with which Americans found new approaches to old problems were regarded by generations of Europeans as an inspiration and a model to be emulated.

---

3   See also Weidenfeld 2001: 1–9.
4   Democracy in America, Vol. 1, 1835. Creation of machine-readable version: Electronic Edition deposited and marked-up by ASGRP, the American Studies Programs at the University of Virginia, June 1, 1997.

Ambivalence in the relationship between Europe and America

But ambivalence marked the relationship between Europe and America from the very start. The young American nation saw itself as the polar opposite of a Europe mired in war. It deliberately distanced itself from Europe's traditional jostling for power, its constant military adventures in the service of feudal or absolutist regimes, its rigid class structures and religious intolerance. Right up to the time of the American Civil War, the United States feared—with some justification—that the Europeans would use every opportunity to scuttle the "American experiment" they disliked so much.

In cultural terms, the Americans initially felt extremely inferior to the Europeans, though at the same time they tended to view Europeans as arrogant and conceited. In turn, many in Europe complained about the unsophisticated, direct manner of the Americans, their flouting of European customs, their lack of any social traditions and their largely materialistic approach to life.

Thus, from the outset, America and Europe were aware not only of their differences but also of their mutual attraction and their interdependence. This dialectical tension lent the relationship between these two continents in the early days an intensity and dynamism that waxed as the 19th century waned.

America's debut on the European political stage

Vigilant neutrality without entangling alliances

In foreign policy, the United States long followed the tenets laid down by Thomas Jefferson in his inaugural address as the country's third president in 1801: The United States should avoid being caught up in entangling alliances that could drag the country into a foreign power play. However, this never implied any renunciation of active foreign policy by the United States.

In their dealings with their former mother country, and later in their implementation of the Monroe Doctrine—which declared U.S. opposition to European interference in the Americas especially against the European powers—as well as in the westward and southward expansion of American territory, American politicians in those early days displayed just as much cool calculation, diplomatic skill and determination as their counterparts in Europe.

They soon recognized that if they were to realize the goals of American foreign policy, they would need to exert a calculated influence, particularly on the European states. In just one early example, Thomas Jefferson's purchase of the Louisiana Territory from Napoleon in 1803 for $15 million reflected the skill with which the American leaders exploited the rivalries between France, England and Spain during that period.

Thus, even in the 19th century, the United States was far from indifferent toward the European continent. Its foreign policy cannot be summed up with the simple slogan of isolationism; its posture toward the internal affairs of Europe is better described as one of vigilant neutrality.[5]

Notwithstanding this political neutrality, social contacts across the Atlantic were already flourishing. American academics, particularly at elite universities such as Yale and Harvard, maintained close contacts with their European partners. Tens of thousands of American students attended British—and above all German—universities during the 19th century. The European ideal of education, and the British example in particular, dominated the ideas of the upper classes in America. And economic relations between Europe and America were from the very outset based on close mutual dependence.

By the end of the 19th century, increasing worldwide economic and social interdependence, together with the exponential growth in America's economic strength, had reached such a high level that America began to regard political intervention in the global arena as increasingly necessary. At this stage, the American economy was already outperforming that of any European nation. At the turn of the century, for example, the United States was producing five times as much steel as Great Britain, and American wheat exports were becoming an increasing problem for Europe, in particular for German producers. Europe tried to defend itself by introducing customs barriers. The United States responded by proclaiming to the world its policy of open doors—that is, free trade.

---

5   On the historical dimension of the interplay of political self-image and foreign policy dealings, cf. Nau 2002: 60–85. On the connection between American ideology and foreign policy, see also Dittgen 1998: 71–78.

Thus, political action on the world stage, as far as the United States was concerned, was primarily a matter of tackling the traditional European powers, which were once again expanding globally during the age of imperialism. For their part, the European states regarded the full-fledged economic and political power of America as the first step toward that country's involvement in world politics and renewed their efforts to get the United States on their side. They were particularly keen to use the United States as a counterbalance to their rivals in Europe—and hence also as a balancing factor within the old continent.

Intervention for the idea of a free world

The years between 1890 and 1917, when America entered World War I, thus saw the United States becoming inexorably involved in European politics—albeit gradually and by fits and starts. In 1898, the United States waged war for the first time against a European nation (Spain)[6] and outside its own hemisphere (in the Philippines), that is, outside the confines of the Monroe Doctrine.[7]

In 1900, a contingent of American troops was sent overseas as part of the international force that crushed the Boxer Rebellion in Beijing. Later, in 1906, U.S. President Theodore Roosevelt actively intervened to achieve a peaceful solution of the Moroccan crisis—the first example of American mediation in a region that had traditionally been part of the European sphere of influence.[8]

Another point already decided by this time was the question of which side the United States would favor when it did intervene in Europe. Since 1895, Great Britain had been working determinedly to build a strategic alliance with the United States—and in doing so had displayed considerable willingness to compromise. A crucial factor in the American decision to side with the British and the Entente was the fear of a European continent dominated by Germany—that is, the traditional concern over maintaining a balance of power in Europe. But also at play was a new criterion that remains a central element of

6   See Adams 2000: 36–39
7   See on this point Dittgen 1998: 63.
8   On U.S. foreign policy from 1898 to 1914, see Adams 2000: 36–39.

American policy to this day: An entry into war in Europe purely in order to maintain the balance of power would have been difficult to square with the Jeffersonian imperative of avoiding entangling alliances.

The American public, moreover, regarded such an approach as too defensive and irreconcilable with the history of the new world. America was founded on the principles of universal freedom and equality. The United States did not traditionally feel obliged to export its model, but from the very start the nation laid claim to being a worldwide beacon for the new ideas of the Enlightenment.

Thus, President Woodrow Wilson's essential argument for America's entry into World War I and thereby into European politics was not that American economic or political interests were under threat, but rather that the basic values of the American dream of freedom and self-determination were endangered on the very continent where those values had been born and with which the United States was always most closely bound.

Seen from this perspective, the natural ally for America in Europe was the liberal-democratic social system in Britain, which was perceived as locked in a struggle for survival against the autocratic, expansionist state of Germany. Only by reinterpreting a war that had emerged from the traditional approach to power politics—by reframing it as a conflict over the enforcement of basic democratic values— were American politicians able to justify U.S. involvement in this war to the American public. Because Theodore Roosevelt had taken the first steps toward reinterpreting the classic ban on intervention, turning the Monroe Doctrine into a U.S. duty to intervene, this reinterpretation is now known as the Roosevelt Corollary.[9]

Of course, reinterpretation also meant reshaping the policy framework. America was not pursuing the traditional objectives of its allies, who were mainly interested in a redistribution of power within Europe. The United States was fighting—as Wilson formulated it— "for a universal dominion of right by such a concert of free peoples as shall bring safety and peace to all nations."[10]

---

9 Cf. President Roosevelt's State of the Union address to Congress on December 6, 1904, reprinted in Adams 2000: 38f.
10 Woodrow Wilson's war message, April 2, 1917. Cited in Curti 1991: 661.

In other words: America was prepared to guarantee the security of the free nations of Europe with its own military might, provided the Europeans responded by giving up their traditional war diplomacy based on undemocratic decisions and by building—among themselves and together with the United States—a society based on democratic values.

Underpinning this political perception was the unshaken American belief that, in a world liberated from state control of the economic and social spheres, American interests would prevail "naturally" within a system of unrestrained competition.

This aim anchored U.S. policy regarding Europe throughout the entire 20th century. In the wake of World War II, it was the crucial precondition for the founding of NATO as well as for U.S. support for the creation of the European Economic Union. Thus, the United States played a decisive role in ensuring that the originally European ideas of freedom, equality and self-determination—which 80 years before were still regarded as an alien element in international relations—have prevailed as the basic principles of foreign policy, first in Western Europe and today also in Central and Eastern Europe.[11]

The lessons of the interwar period—
Europe and America in the twenties and thirties

U.S. involvement without commitment

The vision of an increasing integration of democratic nations suffered a severe setback following World War I. The U.S. Congress vetoed the accession of the United States to the organization regarded as the central instrument for creating a new world order—the League of Nations—even though its approach and organization were strongly influenced by American ideas. Without the involvement of what was by then the world's leading economic and political power, this model of a universal body for the maintenance of peace was doomed to failure.

The repercussions of this withdrawal of America from Europe are felt to this day, with the ever-looming threat of American isolationism

---

11 On the foreign policy elements of America's development from colony to super-power, see also Cameron 2002: 1–12.

invoked on both sides of the Atlantic when even trivial differences between Europeans and Americans arise.

What tends to be forgotten is that despite a temporary drop in the intensity of political cooperation between Europe and the United States during the interwar period, the social, the cultural, and above all the economic links across the Atlantic continued to increase. And even in the political sphere, relations remained extremely active.[12]

At an early stage, the Americans took a leading role in the task of economic reconstruction in Europe. Aware of the high level of economic interdependence, U.S. economists quickly realized that a rapid recovery from the war-induced recession in Europe would be a key element for ensuring the health of the American economy. Unlike France and Britain, the United States endeavored to put Germany in a position where it could pay the reparations required under the Treaty of Versailles.

The Americans were convinced that without economic stabilization in Germany, peace would not return to Europe. Thus, American bankers such as Charles Dawes and Owen Young played a leading role in regulating the financial structures for European reconstruction with American capital and the support of the American government.[13] This meant, among other things, that even at this stage the dollar also started to assume the role of reserve currency in Europe.

In political terms, the U.S. government was also extremely active in Europe during this period, making full use of its increased influence. The principle of most-favored-nation status, that is, liberalization of trade, was expanded further in Europe. And behind the scenes, American diplomats were working feverishly to obtain a peaceful settlement within Europe. In addition, America launched new initiatives in the sphere of disarmament, including the Briand-Kellogg Pact of 1928, whose signatories renounced war as a means of pursuing national objectives and committed themselves to peaceful resolution of conflicts.[14] America had become a fixture on the European political scene.

At the same time, the 1920s and 1930s witnessed a social turning point: American ideas and products began to dominate European

---

12 On the overall course of transatlantic relations since the end of World War I, see also Forndran 1990: 9–36.

13 For more on the Dawes-Young Plan, see, for example, Ritschl 2002 and Holz 1997.

14 For more on the Brian-Kellogg Pact, see Buchheit 1998 and Kneeshaw 1991.

mass culture in a way that continues to this day. Hollywood movies conquered Europe, while the American entertainment industry, American music and American dances began to spread throughout the world. Europe was flooded with American consumer goods, which set new standards for European products too. By the mid-1920s, the United States had become the world's greatest exporting nation, and the Americans increasingly began to see themselves as the one and only source of modern ideas—especially for Europe.

Renationalization of monetary and economic policy

In the 1930s, the global economic crisis led to a temporary plateau in Euro-American relations. The economic and financial order painstakingly built up with American help during the 1920s collapsed and was replaced by a renationalization of monetary and economic policy that also permeated other areas of political life.

It became clear that a policy of involvement without commitment, as pursued by the Europeans and Americans in the period following World War I, would not sustain a durable transatlantic community. Despite close social ties and a broad range of political contacts and joint projects, the Europeans and Americans did not have the strength to resist the centrifugal forces resulting from the collapse of the Versailles order.

However, it would be wrong to attach all the blame for this failure to the United States and to ascribe it to American reluctance to assume a leading role within Europe. At the time, the European states regarded possible American dominance in Europe with the utmost suspicion. They did not yet have any experience with international financial institutions. And as the international economic crisis deepened, the Europeans too were dominated by a tendency to cut themselves off from the outside world. There was a general fear that excessively close and unguarded cooperation with the United States would lead to the crisis being solved at Europe's expense.

The underlying reason for the crisis at that time was not the way the United States had seemingly turned its back on Europe. The establishment of a new order in Europe failed because neither the European nations nor the United States were yet ready for the vision, put forward by the United States after World War I, of a transatlantic (and, ideally, worldwide) community of democratic states that would renounce military rivalries once and for all and agree on credible guarantees for their common security.[15]

Building the transatlantic community after World War II

A second chance to realize a vision

Thus, when the nations of Europe and the United States came to tackle the question of restructuring the transatlantic relationship following World War II, they could look back on a rich history of common political as well as economic interdependence. On both sides of the Atlantic, there was a deeply rooted understanding that international strategies for problem-solving could succeed only through transatlantic cooperation. The vision of a community of states based on democratic principles had appeared on the horizon, but proof was still outstanding that this was feasible in reality.

After the National Socialists launched their war in Europe, it became evident that the idea had fallen on fertile ground. Building on its experience during World War I, and drawing upon President Wilson's concept of universal peace, the United States seized the initiative and in 1941 formulated the Atlantic Charter together with Britain.

This document not only attests to the will of the democratic nations to resist German aggression but also, in principle, outlines a vision similar to the American vision back in 1917: the creation of a free order based on the self-determination of nations, a secure peace and a liberal, nondiscriminatory world trade system.

In 1945, unlike in 1918, steps were taken to realize this vision. Two phenomena crucially influenced this new approach. First, the appalling destruction and atrocities of World War II demonstrated that the traditional European policy of maintaining a balance of power was both practically and morally defunct. And second, the growing Soviet threat that emerged soon after the end of the war brought home to the states of the Western world the urgency of developing a genuinely common defense and security policy.

15 See also Junker 1999: 121–143.

Nevertheless, the inaugurators of the postwar order—leaders such as George Marshall, Robert Schuman and Konrad Adenauer—met with considerable resistance both at home and abroad as they set out to establish the Western alliance. In Germany, the idea of irreversible ties to the West raised controversy because this could be interpreted as abandoning any possibility of reunification. This irreversible commitment to the United States also drew criticism in other western European states, as did the de facto admission of the recent enemy, Germany, to the new peace order on equal terms. And in the United States, such permanent and binding guarantees of security for Europe met with dispute simply because the idea was so new.

The formation of the Western alliance—first of all NATO, but also its economic-political correlate in Europe, the European Economic Community—was nevertheless anything but a foregone conclusion. It is only the success of these new structures in the course of the postwar and Cold War years that allows us to see them now as the only possible outcome of World War II. Ultimately, the credit for creating this new order must go to the vision, determination and practical skills displayed by the postwar generation of politicians, who recognized and grasped the unique opportunity for a fresh start and ensured its success through their domestic and foreign policies.

The most far-reaching consequences of this reorientation were undoubtedly felt in German foreign policy. The Federal Republic of Germany had to completely redefine the basic coordinates of its policy—abandoning the uncertainties of vacillating positions on issues, relinquishing all go-it-alones and nationalistic policies, and making a clear commitment to cooperation in stabilizing Western freedoms. Thus, for the first time ever, the country's internal order and external alignment matched each other. Political culture had become the compass with which the Germans in the Federal Republic mapped their position within the world. And this position was, and indeed remains, one of integration—a term with many connotations: incorporation into the Western alliance, German-American friendship, European unity.[16]

The ties thus created between Germany and America, some of which were based on formal treaties, came as a package deal. The Federal Republic definitively invested all of its interests and its poten-

16 For more on this topic, see Hanrieder 1995, 4–12.

tial in the common Western strategy. In turn, the nations of the West, led by the Americans, committed themselves not to interfere in all matters—including the German Question.

U.S. involvement in Europe after World War II

The United States had many reasons for involvement in Europe after World War II—reasons of global policy, security and economics. Towering over them all, however, was a central political and cultural motive: The United States sought to defend its own dream of itself in Europe. What roused its emotions was not a distant, largely unknown continent. Rather, it was the fact that Europe mirrored the American soul that motivated American society. Amid the teeming heterogeneity and marked segmentation of American society, there are few cultural symbols to cement it. The goal of establishing an ethos of freedom worldwide stands as a pillar of domestic politics.

In Berlin, America defended its dream of the new world. Berlin triggered emotions that had an extremely important impact in American politics. Consequently, the fall of the Berlin Wall unleashed a groundswell of sentiment that was at least as strong in the United States as in Germany itself. For decades, Germany and Europe could always be invoked as a way of rousing emotions on the American political scene. This keystone of domestic politics made possible an extraordinary tangible and intangible commitment to the generation-spanning existence of a security alliance. In the United States, no complicated theory of international politics was needed. The alliance was imperative to the American society's image of itself.

The role played by the Americans in the historic task of rebuilding Western Europe after World War II went far beyond mere tangible investments. America gave the defeated in Europe an opportunity to regain their self-respect—and earned gratitude in return. But anyone who makes such a strong intangible commitment inevitably becomes more sensitive to perceived irritants: when yesterday's protégé begins to assert its status as a partner, for example, or when support for European unity does more to create an economic competitor than to reduce political tensions—or when in the eyes of many Germans their much-admired role model overindulges in calculated tactics in pursuit of world power.

36

The stages of the alliance—
from overemphasis of the positive to mature cooperation

Phases in a shifting relationship

Even after the postwar order had found its footing, the development of the transatlantic alliance did not proceed without interruption and internal conflict. Initially, the main focus was on trying out this unprecedented level of cooperation and taking the steps needed, particularly the internal measures, to ensure that it would last. Just how difficult this was in some instances can be seen from the German debate on rearmament and NATO membership. In addition to this, the balance vis-à-vis the Warsaw Pact was by no means as stable as it was to become in the 1960s and 1970s, when the policy of peaceful coexistence was accepted on all sides.

First phase: Playing up the positive

In the 1950s, on both sides of the Atlantic, positive aspects were played up. Particularly in West Germany, the United States was seen as an absolute model, the ideal to follow. A tendency to imitate took over, and the shared antipathy toward Communism intensified this turning to the West. Across the Atlantic, Europe after the Marshall Plan was regarded as the product of the American dream at work. America, with its dynamic economic strength and missionary zeal for a free, democratic and modern society, assisted at the rebirth of Europe after the American model.

During these years, the Federal Republic of Germany, in particular, was regarded as a sort of miniature United States. Just as the U.S. public imagined East Germany to be a Russian Germany, so they saw West Germany as American and good—"our Germany." The rebuilding of German democracy was viewed as an American re-importation of the European Enlightenment. The successful linkage of stable democracy with strong economic growth made West Germany look like the embodiment of American ideals.

Second phase: Dramatizing the negative

The second phase of German-American postwar relations, characterized by dramatization of the negative, began with the end of the 1960s. Culturally, the United States became for many the quintessential villain, the visible expression of everything wrong with the existing order. Vietnam symbolized a war-hungry aggressiveness; Watergate symbolized a political and moral decline; fast-food temples and soap operas were symbols of the abandonment of cultural legitimacy. These were the widespread perceptions of the United States among European intellectuals.[17]

European self-confidence, now coming into its own, spurred on such views. But at the same time, the loss of the ideal role model triggered an identity debate among Europeans. Differing opinions about the extent of European enlargement and the creation of a European political order went hand in hand with divergent views of the transatlantic relationship in general and the security alliance in particular, as well as the East-West conflict. The debate about Europe's future role in the world had begun.[18]

The Soviet Union's invasion of Afghanistan in December 1979 marked another important turning point in this phase. In the context of the Cold War, the invasion caused consternation in the Western world; it was seen as an indirect threat, especially to the situation in the Persian Gulf. But apart from diplomatic protests, the Western powers took no action, leaving the people of Afghanistan to mount their own defense against the aggressor.

Third phase: Transition to sober realism

In the 1980s, the third phase saw the playing down of both the negative and the positive. Europe no longer admired the United States as a glorified role model or rejected it as an anti-power. Henceforth both partners held a sober appreciation of the possibilities and limitations of transatlantic cooperation. The awareness of parallel interests as well

17 For social and political development in the US through the mid-70s, see Berg 1999, 144–168.
18 See also Hanrieder 1995, 285–307.

as disagreements, of commonalities as well as differences, became sharper.

The collapse of the Warsaw Pact, which presented completely new challenges, reinforced this tendency toward sober realism in transatlantic relations. The downfall of a onetime opponent was not celebrated as a triumph; rather, it spurred immediate action on the concrete tasks of political and economic reconstruction in the eastern region of the formerly divided continent. Sobriety also was necessary because the interests of the individual partners in the Western alliance were hardly identical.

Thus, German unification would have proceeded far less swiftly and cooperatively had the Americans not supported it so actively, even in the face of doubts on the part of their Western European partners. Working closely with their German colleagues, American political figures were the driving force behind the consultations and negotiations that led to German unification. Underpinning this close political collaboration were cordial ties among top politicians and government officials, mutual political trust and the clear common goal of a unified Germany firmly anchored in the Western alliance.

New issues and a different atmosphere

But in the decade after the Cold War subsided, German unification was not the only issue on which views in the West diverged. Different emphases also emerged in attitudes toward Russia, in opinions on who should bear the burden of economic reconstruction in Eastern Europe, and—most strikingly—in responses to the crisis in the former Yugoslavia precipitated by the collapse of the Eastern bloc.

On the other hand, many historic differences within the alliance dwindled, among them the debate on the instruments required for a common security policy that had raged during the 1980s. The regular protests against the stationing of American troops in various states in Europe also died down. Even the dispute about sharing the cost of a common defense policy had lost its urgency.

In addition, the fall of the Soviet Union and the fading of the immediate security threat turned the attention of both Europe and the United States toward their domestic problems with unprecedented intensity. Since then, the EU has faced central challenges on parallel tracks: on the one hand a deepening of integration, and on the other the expansion eastward that was formalized on May 1, 2004. In the United States, before the terrorist attacks of September 11, 2001, the presidential and congressional elections from 1992 to 2000 symbolized a growing dominance of domestic issues on the American political agenda, at times totally excluding foreign policy.

At the start of the new century, differences once considered peripheral surged to the center of transatlantic political awareness. These differences focused on such things as the campaign against international terrorism, varying reactions to crises in countries outside the alliance, nuclear proliferation and the control of weapons of mass destruction, but also the recurring transatlantic conflicts over trade and global environmental politics.

After the election of George W. Bush in 2000, these differences came to a head. The year 2001 brought considerable tensions regarding—among other things—the outrage over the U.S. rejection of the Kyoto Protocol on climate protection and the U.S. withdrawal of its signature on the statute for the International Criminal Court.

The first meeting between German chancellor Gerhard Schröder and President George W. Bush in March 2001 could not have been more revealing. Just a few hours before the chancellor's arrival, Bush delivered a public rebuff to his guest's key interests. With unaccustomed directness, the American president even emphasized the disagreement during a brief photo session in the Oval Office—and Schröder issued a retort. Images from the past come tellingly to mind: Ronald Reagan's visit to the Hambacher Schloss, his speech at the Berlin Wall, the scenes of casual camaraderie that Helmut Kohl and Bill Clinton staged over mounds of pasta at Filomena in Georgetown. What a contrast to the cool detachment since the year 2000—a reserve that threatened to deepen with the reelection of George W. Bush in November 2004, particularly since Europeans had more or less openly backed the Democratic candidate John Kerry.

The political elite on both sides played a significant role as the atmosphere of the transatlantic relationship changed. The generation of Reagan, Thatcher and Kohl had constructed its political worldview in the unambiguous order of the Cold War. Antagonism to the East and cordial relations in the West were two sides of the same coin. Transatlantic solidarity formed the cornerstone of security and freedom in Western Europe. From that arose a framework, at once emotional and programmatic, that gave politics an orientation and stable foundation beyond the interests of the day. The political leaders of Western Europe were schooled in grateful friendship toward the United States, and the political elite across the Atlantic—from Henry Kissinger to Vernon Walters—exuded cordiality in return.

Broad segments of today's generation of politicians on both sides of the Atlantic experienced a different political socialization. Opposition to the fossilization of that founding era of transatlantic relations dominated their youth. From that opposition arose a new mental filter—not an anti-Atlantic mindset, but certainly one that coolly considered how to weigh and balance the factors of international politics in any given situation. The margins for action have widened. Those who calmly stand their ground against the United States earn bonus points in Europe today.[19]

After September 11, 2001: Common threats and shared responses

With the terrorist attacks of September 11, 2001, transatlantic relations have once again acquired an overarching bond that takes the form of a common threat. International terrorism has taken center stage as the dominant security problem of the Western world. However, such a new common security threat has not summoned an automatic commitment to reviving a shared security policy in the transatlantic alliance, as the most recent differences in Iraq policies demonstrate. On the contrary: The different security policy responses to the threat of terrorism and to the constraints of international law have brought a new dimension to mutual problem-solving for the transatlantic partners.

Yes, the Euro-American security community remains in place, but without the structures, the presence and the mentality of a highly integrated defense organization that is always combat-ready, poised to repel a full-scale attack. Yes, the political community still bridges the Atlantic, but without any special sensitivity toward the course of transatlantic relations. Yes, Western societies still hold shared values and a common identity, but they have yet to define their commonality and their specific contribution when it comes to the new issues in international politics.

19 Weidenfield 2001, 1–9.

The time is past when American involvement in Europe stood as a social imperative and transatlantic cooperation indisputably held sway. Berlin has shrunk to just another place on the map. What American dream could be realized in Europe today? In earlier times, the mayor of Berlin could not have visited Washington without seeing the president. Today, no suitably high-ranking officials have time to talk—and why should they? Under the imperative of U.S. domestic politics, they may make time for European investors creating American jobs. But the traditional playing out of roles on the political stage, inspired by the image of partners in the trenches doing battle against dictators, no longer resonates with the population on either side of the Atlantic—and that was true even before the United States went to war against Iraqi dictator Saddam Hussein in what was arguably a violation of international law.

U.S. multilateralism à la carte

Even now, the Europeans have not fully recognized the consequences of this fundamental shift. Time and again, American decisions come as a surprise. From the Iraq policy to missile defense to climate protection—in the United States, domestic politics rule the day. The constraints set by domestic politics define the terms for all foreign policy matters. This has not necessarily spawned a new American isolationism or anti-European mindset. Europe has simply been booted from its earlier privileged position into a more normal reality based on national interests. Cooperation is now sought in an à la carte multilateralism, case by case.

At the same time, the Americans often show very little understanding for European politics. With its strict focus on results, the United States fails to appreciate the protracted, complex decision-making processes of European integration. From the American partner's point of view, such procedures are too ponderous, inefficient and slow. Every European announcement of an important new step toward integration is thus viewed with a high degree of skepticism. When, contrary to expectations, such steps actually take place—from economic and monetary union to common defense policy—Washington's skepticism threatens to turn into distrust.

Conversely, the European side also has a limited understanding of the conditions and possibilities of the American partner. In the

1990s, for example, when the Balkan crisis threatened to erupt into war, the Europeans tried to convince Washington to send troops. At first, the Americans resisted; the U.S. public had no interest in the Balkans. Experiencing American disinterest for the first time in decades, the Europeans were shocked.

Later, when the American media sent images of Balkan atrocities across the Atlantic, the political environment in the United States changed, leading the Americans to intervene militarily. Not content with minor tasks, they took center stage. The Europeans, elbowed into a merely ornamental role, thus received their second shock. The lesson they drew from this—the need to build up their own military capacity—was in turn misunderstood in Washington.

Similar misunderstandings arose from the war against the Taliban in Afghanistan. On October 2, 2001, at the instigation of the Europeans, NATO invoked article 5 of its charter for the first time in its history. Nevertheless, the Americans did not make use of NATO's military capacity in Afghanistan. Instead, the United States requested that the alliance take over mere odd jobs like the monitoring of American air space. The United States conducted the military operation in Afghanistan (Operation Enduring Freedom). But for many European states, the breaking point came when the United States launched its war in Iraq. Again, the Europeans were taken aback and felt snubbed by the Americans' national decision.

Europe in an emancipation trap

The cases of the Balkans, Afghanistan und Iraq illustrate a basic point: Europe is freeing itself of American patronage without having learned how to act in the world of international politics, and thus finds itself in an emancipation trap. Europe must develop an independent method of proceeding without a strategic concept or an order of priorities. Europe can no longer sail along in America's wake, but it is not yet able to chart and steer its own course without American guidance.

The resulting ambiguity in European behavior visibly bewilders the Americans. In response, Washington is falling back on old habits: either to go its own way or seek specific deals with individual European powers. Thus, now as before, the supranational integration of Europe tends to raise question marks on both sides of the Atlantic.

With the severity of a purist, Washington is only interested in one thing: What can Europe contribute? How much can its technological prowess, its economic performance, its security policy be relied on? Where can it share the burden of global political responsibility? The United States will take serious notice of Europe only where Europe can deliver the results Washington wants.

In the 1990s, the bond between Europe and the United States survived on its capital, the fund of agreement and trust built up in the setting of Western cooperation over previous decades. For the future, Europe and the United States must replenish that capital by forming a new community. Unless they can renew their partnership, the danger looms of a cultural split in which the personal experiences, the structures and cooperative pathways, the successes and the lessons of the past are lost.

Thus, before one can assess the scope for a new start in transatlantic relations at the dawn of the 21st century, it is necessary to take a look at the present domestic situation of the partners involved. To what extent, given their domestic political agendas, will the European Union and the United States be in a position to jointly assume international responsibilities? How can the dissonances in the transatlantic relationship be resolved? What forms, what quality of transatlantic engagement will the public on either side of the Atlantic be prepared to accept, now that a new and acute threat has arisen?

3 The United States at the beginning of the 21st century

After the East-West conflict ended, the United States was the only remaining superpower. This required the United States to set a new course in both foreign and domestic policy and redefine its role in global events. This chapter describes how the United States redirected its foreign policy after the Cold War, its reaction to the September 11, 2001 terrorist attacks in both foreign and domestic policy, and its economic and social problems at home. The end of the chapter illuminates the world power's outlook for the future.

U.S. foreign policy after the Cold War

A world power moving in a new direction

The United States knows it is the only remaining world power since the fall of the Soviet Union. This reduces pressure on the United States to enter into lasting alliances. But even a single superpower needs supporters—so it seems useful to have at least occasional partners in Europe, Asia and the Arab world. Then burdens can be shared and partnerships established for stability. But these networks are neither as firmly established nor as long-term as they had been. They are meant to be functional and to serve selected purposes. Of course, Europeans must bear a large part of the burden of rebuilding the Balkans, Afghanistan and Iraq; of course, Europeans must share the financial burdens of the Middle East. But strategic decisions fall on the shoulders of the sole world power.

There are few equal competitors with a similar ambition for power. The United States no longer views Russia as a world power; its economy is still too weak, its social policy stagnant and its military rusty.

Up until now, India and Japan have only reached the level of influential medium-sized powers. Though the European Union has the economic capital and infrastructure of a world power, it lacks efficient military and security politics as well as strategic thinking. "Europe has to get its act together" is the general sentiment. Only then will the United States take it seriously as a strategic partner.

China—as a power that could rise to equal stature over the medium term—had been the focus of the United States' attention for some time. This focus helped to define the development of a constructive strategic partnership in 1997 under President Clinton, who sought to intensify the bilateral dialogue on nuclear proliferation. This was a big step in the bilateral relations, particularly after the tensions in the Taiwan Straits in 1995/1996, which almost led to a military confrontation between China and the United States. The United States formulated its strategy of comprehensive engagement on the assumption that China would develop into an economic and military superpower over the next 10 to 20 years, establishing closer ties with the United States. For this reason, it would be best to include China in global strategies right from the start.[20]

Domestic policy priorities

Despite this new foreign policy challenge, domestic affairs dominated the political agenda in Washington during the 1990s. For the 1991 Gulf War, to avoid giving the impression of a unilateral cowboy mentality, President George H. W. Bush summoned support from the Soviet Union and the U.N. Security Council and put together the largest possible international coalition. At war's end, everything seemed to indicate that the United States—fortified by its moral and military triumph—would vigorously devote its energy to building the new world order proclaimed by President George H. W. Bush. But the United States savored this victory only briefly.

During the 1992 presidential election campaign, Bill Clinton issued the constant reminder: "It's the economy, stupid." He accused the Bush administration of spending exorbitant amounts on defense and focusing too strongly on foreign policy. At the same time, a wide

20 For more on this topic, see Möller 2000, 65–86.

range of publications fueled the American public's fears of falling into obscurity on the world political scene after the demise of the Soviet Union.

Although Clinton was confronted with three major foreign policy issues right at the start of his term—the collapse of state systems in Haiti, the violent and total disintegration of the state in Somalia and the intensifying conflict in the Balkans—the presidential and congressional elections in the 1990s pointed American policy in a completely different direction. The United States finally had to tackle domestic problems that had grown to massive proportions over decades.

Clinton set his priorities on expanding democracy and free trade and preparing for the economic challenges of globalization. To that end, he relied on multilateral organizations—but left no doubts that the United States was perfectly willing to take on issues alone if necessary. The military disaster in Mogadishu in 1993/1994 contributed significantly to American aversion to U.S troop deployments on foreign soil. Critics accused Clinton of not even having a foreign policy strategy.[21]

Under Clinton, the full dimensions of homegrown problems that had festered for decades were fully recognized for the first time. This change in perception was signaled by an almost total concentration of American policy on the domestic agenda; many policy areas even slipped into provincialism. The domestic policy changes in the United States also caused a significant shift of emphasis in foreign policy. Word had already spread that calls for eliminating development assistance for the Third World were a perfectly viable campaign tactic for both Democratic and Republican congressional candidates in rural areas. Faced with the ambitious domestic policy agenda of the new Republican-controlled Congress, the electorate regarded any foreign contacts cultivated by members of Congress as highly suspect, because they distracted attention from what were perceived as the real tasks at hand.

Domestic policy challenges determine U.S. foreign policy

Even more dramatic than the impact of this shift in priorities on American foreign policy was the impact of the shift in thinking that

21   See also Cameron 2002, 13–29.

ensued. Starting in 1994, influential forces, particularly the congressional leadership, committed to a radical reinterpretation of American foreign policy, using domestic challenges to steer foreign policy initiatives as well. Just as in domestic affairs, they regarded the United States as unnecessarily constrained by excessive bureaucracy and inefficiency in pursuit of foreign policy, and they adopted the view that U.S. policy abroad had drifted too far from the ideas and interests of the American people.

In a parallel development, cooperation with international organizations came under critical scrutiny. Here too, a campaign of radical reinterpretation was launched. If the explicit aim of the new domestic policy was to reclaim America's pioneer status in terms of its internal structures, then this "America first" policy—as it translated to foreign affairs—meant giving priority to national interests over multilateral obligations.

The first target of this approach was the United Nations. The United Nations was largely blamed for a number of American foreign policy mishaps, ostensibly because the United States was bogged down in multilateral decision-making structures. This accounted for its unsuccessful involvement in Somalia under the U.N. flag, its contradictory maneuvers in Haiti, and its share in the failure of U.N. politics in the former Yugoslavia. The long-term consequences of this trend unfolded when the United States chose to go it alone in Afghanistan and Iraq.

Following this line of logic, the U.S. Congress concentrated after 1994 on restricting the scope for government cooperation with the United Nations. Among other things, Congress decided that in future no U.S. troops would be deployed in military operations under foreign command—which primarily meant under U.N. command. This was linked with a generally more restrictive doctrine regarding the deployment of American forces for peacekeeping missions on foreign soil.

Foreign policy managed to edge back into the spotlight of political Washington only after the U.S. intervention in Yugoslavia and Clinton's focus on the conflicts in Northern Ireland and the Middle East toward the end of his second term of office. However, this intermezzo ended with the election of George W. Bush to the presidency in November 2000.

When George W. Bush took office in January 2001, a number of well-known foreign policy experts joined the U.S. government as well. Bush roused considerable attention by naming two African-Americans to prominent foreign policy positions: Condoleezza Rice as National Security Advisor and Colin Powell as Secretary of State. Rice, a member of the national security team under George H. W. Bush, was a professor of international relations and provost of the renowned Stanford University. Powell had served as national security advisor under President Ronald Reagan and had become well known as a general and chairman of the Joint Chiefs of Staff during the 1991 Gulf War.

Bush's team also included Donald Rumsfeld as secretary of defense, a post he had held from 1975 to 1977 under President Gerald Ford, and Richard (Dick) Cheney as vice president. Cheney had served as secretary of defense under President George H. W. Bush and was brought on board to help shape the significant features of the second Bush president's foreign policy.

The structural transformation of American foreign policy under George W. Bush began not on September 11, 2001, but as soon as he took office in January 2001. Within its first few months, his administration embarked on a collision course with Clinton's foreign policy. Clinton's multilateralism gave way to a new unilateralism that pushed U.S. national interests into the foreground. Bush declined further political engagement in the Middle East and Northern Ireland, announced his rejection of the Kyoto Protocol on greenhouse gas emissions, suspended all official talks with North Korea, forged ahead on the National Missile Defense program despite international protest, single-handedly withdrew from the ABM Treaty with Russia and nullified Clinton's signature on the statute for the International Criminal Court—an unprecedented event in international law. Scaling back American engagement in the Middle East and fueling the conflict between China and Taiwan were also new elements of Bush's foreign policy.

Catchphrases such as "new realism" (Condoleezza Rice) and "multilateralism à la carte" (Richard Haass, State Department director for policy planning) made the rounds. This new American nationalism garnered Bush the firm support of Republican hard-liners, but it also elicited harsh criticism from domestic policy opponents and international partners. The European press portrayed Bush as an arrogant cowboy devoid of any sense for foreign policy, making an impression more with verbal incoherence than political savvy.

The United States' claim to leadership with a new focus

How can this perception of the U.S. political leadership, and first and foremost the president, be explained? It must be noted that during the 1990s, the national interests of the United States clearly took precedence over its global security responsibilities in crisis regions around the world. This was accompanied by a general re-evaluation of international troop deployments, including the American forces stationed in Europe.

This shift in foreign policy coordinates has sometimes been misinterpreted as party politics, that is to say a phenomenon that emerged solely due to the Republican majority in Congress. In reality, it speaks to a generational changing of the guard in both parties. Virtually all the recently elected members of Congress, whether Democrat or Republican, peppered their election campaigns with attacks on what they saw as the Washington establishment's misguided foreign policy goals—at least until September 11. This trend of generation change will be strengthened in the future. The political circle committed to the transatlantic cause is being replaced by a new group of pragmatic politicians.

Proponents of this new American foreign policy strategy vehemently reject accusations from the European side that they are promoting a new U.S. isolationism. On the contrary: They see it as a matter of reasserting America's claim to leadership in the world, freed from the encumbrances of both American government bureaucracy and multilateral commitments. Thus, proponents of this strategy can best be described as unilateralists.[22]

However, the very fact that the United States needs to concentrate more on domestic economic and social problems underscores the need for renewed foreign policy efforts to ensure that the burden of American international involvement—which is as necessary as ever—can be shared more efficiently with its allies and partners.

---

22 For a detailed description of the different theoretical concepts of U.S. foreign policy, see Nau 2002, 43–59.

Despite this concentration on domestic issues, the American public has always reacted acutely to foreign policy blunders, since these represent the most public contradiction of America's ongoing claim to set an example for the world. Therefore, it is unlikely that the United States will retreat from world politics or restrict its involvement to a narrower geopolitical sphere.

Nevertheless, the sheer extent of the present upheaval in U.S. domestic politics should not be underestimated. For the first time since the New Deal in the 1930s, broad segments of the population seem receptive to change in the domestic policy paradigm. Many Americans seem to regard pruning back the state apparatus, which the Keynesian approach of President Theodore Roosevelt and his successors apparently allowed to run rampant, as the cure-all to revive the American dream.

But when they came, the terrorist attacks of September 11 and subsequent calls for a global war on terror turned domestic and foreign policy priorities upside down and inside out.

The foreign policy agenda after September 11

Both U.S. foreign policy and its reception in domestic and foreign media changed abruptly with the terrorist attacks of September 11, 2001. The attacks radically altered the political scene in the United States. America had been attacked on its home territory for the first time and suffered some 3,000 casualties—the heaviest toll of lives lost in a single day since the 19th century Civil War battle of Gettysburg.

This was a traumatic experience for the United States, the world power. Even before the attacks, speculation had swirled through political circles that terrorist organizations were not only striving to obtain weapons of mass destruction, but were also willing and able to attack the United States on its home turf. A series of terrorist attacks on U.S. foreign installations, including the 1998 bombing of the U.S. embassies in Kenya and Tanzania and the 2000 attack on the U.S.S. Cole in the port of Aden, served as harbingers of worse to come. In response, President Clinton placed international terrorism at the top of America's international political agenda.

But now the very heart of the U.S. homeland had become the scene of international terrorism. At the same time, the technological asymmetry of the attack shocked the American public: Terrorists armed with box-cutters had transformed civilian aircraft into flying bombs, rendering all the high-tech weapons of the U.S. military powerless.

The attack on September 11 unleashed powerful forces, inflicted painful wounds and drew the public's gaze into the abyss of real dangers once hidden in the shadows. The American public reacted with bewildered grief, anger, doubt, fear and a groundswell of patriotism. Buoyed by these emotions, President Bush declared war on international terrorism on September 20, 2001. The guilty parties were swiftly identified: Osama bin Laden and his al-Qaida terror network.

Around the world, people expected a rapid and powerful military response against terrorists and countries that supported them. But military strategists in the United States knew that concentrating firepower on individual terrorists would not achieve American objectives. The Bush administration thus did not strike back immediately. Instead, Bush pledged the American people to a long battle waged on many levels and on many fronts, with many outcomes measurable only far down the road.

U.S. reaction to the terror attack of September 11

Criticism of the policies and the person of President Bush was hushed in the wake of worldwide shock. But as they planned the political and military campaign against terrorism, the White House and the Pentagon soon realized that they could not win this struggle without the support of other nations. The unilateralism of the Bush government's first nine months had to be replaced—at least for the fight against terror—by a limited multilateralism, a coalition of the willing. However, Bush left no doubt that this new multilateral approach would be oriented clearly to American interests. His definition of multilateralism was simple: You are either with us or against us. He allowed no room for variations on this theme.

With a great deal of diplomatic engagement, the United States assembled an illustrious coalition in the war on terrorism. Important international actors such as the United Nations, NATO and the European Union, as well as the Organization of American States and the Organization of the Islamic Conference, promptly declared their support. Russia, China, India and Pakistan also sided with the United States. Many countries in Central Asia as well as numerous Arabic nations followed suit.

Bush's blunt dichotomy did not miss its mark as the military operation against the Taliban regime in Afghanistan loomed. The effect of this political pressure was most telling in Pakistan. That Islamic state—a military dictatorship with friendly ties to the Taliban regime and a designated rogue state in possession of nuclear weapons, and hence a likely target of the American war on terror—risked considerable domestic tension to open its airspace to the United States and provide support in the war against the Taliban. In return, Pakistan was spared U.S. aggression and a number of sanctions against the country were lifted. So the "with us or against us" stance could also turn former enemies into new friends.

In foreign policy, the United States responded to the changing constellation after September 11 with a strategy of cooperation à la carte. It chose several partner countries, luring them with money and prestige—even when this meant damaging international organizations that had previously been useful. This applied equally to NATO, the European Union and the United Nations.[23]

The classic imperative "divide et impera" (divide and conquer) had its effect within the European Union. The symbolic culmination of this was the letter of solidarity with the United States signed by the leaders of eight European nations. This letter documented the rift within Europe. Militarily, the United States reacted to the terror attacks by embarking on the long-term restructuring of the Army to a mobile force, rapidly deployable worldwide, and by beefing up its defense budget, set to double to approximately $700 billion by 2007. This would bring defense spending to its highest level in absolute numbers (though not as a percentage of gross domestic product) since the massive armaments buildup under President Ronald Reagan. Though the asymmetrical nature of the threat was recognized, it made no difference to that plan.

In the face of terrorism, the U.S. government proclaimed a new strategy that aimed to make not just U.S. territory but the whole world safer. In this move, Bush quite deliberately played the world power card: In the wake of September 11, the United States as the

23 Bücherl 2003, 55–59.

sole world power had a unique obligation to define and establish a new world order. New challenges demanded a new way of thinking, according to the official document announcing the new doctrine. The first priority must be to fight terrorism and the rogue states that constitute a threat to freedom.

Next to the essential homeland security pillar, the Bush doctrine gave just as much weight to preventive and preemptive strikes as to counter-proliferation efforts and cooperative security measures that included other major powers.[24] However, Bush left no doubt about the United States' willingness to act alone, should other powers choose not to participate. Bush's military reform went hand in hand with Defense Secretary Rumsfeld's statement, "The best defense is a good offense."[25]

U.S. anti-terrorism policy in the case of Iraq

The U.S. policy on Iraq mirrored the foreign policy pursued by the administration in Washington. The tone and policy toward Iraq had already sharpened immediately after George W. Bush took over in the White House. A significant number of political hard-liners led by Defense Secretary Donald Rumsfeld, Vice President Dick Cheney and Deputy Secretary of Defense Paul Wolfowitz—the "hawks" of U.S. foreign policy—promoted a political mission to finish the job left unfinished by the previous Bush administration: the removal of Saddam Hussein.

The terror attacks of September 11 fed the ambitions of these hawks, who placed Saddam Hussein in the camps of terrorist groups and accused him of illegal possession and proliferation of weapons of mass destruction. The political opposition—the doves led by U.S. Secretary of State Colin Powell—not only saw a new war in Iraq as a risky undertaking that could cost the lives of many U.S. soldiers, but also warned that such a mission might very well have to be unilateral, because many allies in the war on terrorism had rejected the idea of an Iraq war early on.

---

24 For the new U.S. national security strategy and homeland security strategy, see: The President of the United States 2002, www.whitehouse.gov/nsc/nss.pdf and Office of Homeland Security 2002, www.whitehouse.gov/homeland/book/nat_strat_hls.pdf (accessed February 1, 2005).
25 Schley 2002.

Although today's situation and state of affairs has disproved the presumption of Iraqi collaboration with the al-Qaida network and possession of weapons of mass destruction, at the time the majority of the American public believed that the United States should proceed militarily against Iraq. Even Congress voted in favor of the President's resolution regarding the course of war, despite some debate over the details. With this support, President Bush was able to embark on his plan for regime change in Iraq even in opposition to the convictions of his allies. And he explicitly gave notice that he was prepared to tackle the problem without the backing of the United Nations if need be.

After France, Russia and China refused to let the U.N. Security Council legitimize a preventive war against Iraq, Bush saw only two options: He could back down and withdraw U.S. troops from the Persian Gulf, which would probably cost the United States its status as a superpower and presumably cost him the presidency as well—or he could follow the dictates of his foreign policy doctrine and go to war with Iraq without the legitimation of international law.

The relatively clear re-election of President George W. Bush in November 2004 confirmed both the foreign policy course pursued by the United States under his leadership and the direction of public sentiment in the war on terrorism. The most important change during the administration's restructuring was the replacement of Secretary of State Colin Powell with Condoleezza Rice, who enjoyed Bush's full confidence and stood—and still stands—by his side on every important issue.

Impact of the Iraq war on transatlantic relations

The Iraq war presented the transatlantic relationship with its greatest challenge since World War II. After the war in Afghanistan, which barely stayed within the bounds of justifiability, the level of misunderstanding between the partners skyrocketed when the United States attacked Iraq. The result was a noticeable chill in the transatlantic partnership, further aggravated by the argument that the United States did not need long-standing partnerships, but rather coalitions of the willing.

President Bush underpinned his military action in Iraq with two assertions: that Iraq possessed weapons of mass destruction and that

Iraq and its dictator, Saddam Hussein, were in collaboration with al-Qaida. Both assertions, supposedly based on intelligence documents, proved false. Hans Blix and his U.N. inspection (UNMOVIC) found no evidence of weapons of mass destruction,[26] and a bipartisan U.S. Senate committee came to the conclusion in July 2004 that the available intelligence reports were not only "proven false, [but] were unreasonable and largely unsupported by the available intelligence."[27]

Throughout the entire deployment period, as the troops massed for war, Germany and France led the majority of European nations in voicing doubts about the reasons given to justify the attack. The U.S. government paid little heed. Slowly, almost stealthily, a rivalry entered the transatlantic relationship and began to take hold.

On one side stand the Americans who support the war, with the impassioned combativeness of George W. Bush and his circle of hard-liners, united in the desire not only to close the chapter on Saddam Hussein, but also to stem the tide of terrorism driven by politics and religion. The U.S. national security strategy spells this out in no uncertain terms when it states that a preemptive military strike is an option even when based only on the mere suspicion of a threat.

On the other side stand the Europeans, whose common foreign and security policy is oriented toward preventing war at all costs—the Europeans who prefer to rely on diplomacy, not force.

Given the number of trouble spots that plague our era of global unrest, this rivalry of perceptions and policies will shadow transatlantic relations for some time to come. And yet—what if rivalry also means the opportunity for a fresh start? What if the rivals could forge new common strategies that turn the politics of world order in a new direction? For this to work, both partners need to take on a share of the responsibility. Their many years of working in partnership toward common goals surely afford the two sides a workable platform for a fresh start.

The Iraq war has made plain the widening rift between the New World and the Old. It did so with particular clarity as U.S. relations with Germany and France took their course. Germans traveling to the United States since the 2002 Bundestag elections encountered a wave of reproach and outrage. Never before had a parliamentary election

26 Blix 2004.
27 International Herald Tribune, 10/11 July 2004, 1 and 6.

abroad aroused such interest in the United States; never had an event such as the German Bundestag election triggered such fury. Nor did the indignation subside after the elections, for the antiwar protests in Germany continued.

Misunderstandings thrive in such a climate. A German visitor to America in late 2002 might as well have landed on another planet, so alien did the situation seem. In short: German-American relations had come to a severe test—as severe as any they have known. Those in Germany who view the U.S. response as short-lived irritation have much to learn about the United States.

These transatlantic misunderstandings took on a particularly distinctive dynamic because the public climate in America at the time was heating up to a feverish pitch. By autumn 2002, with every bit of drama it could muster, the American media had already begun the countdown to war. "Showdown Iraq"—that and other media banners drummed into the public mind the reality of the pending war. No whodunit could have been staged with greater suspense than this period of patriotic tumult. The press reported detailed deployment plans and information on Iraqi customs and traditions—as if briefing every citizen on ethical codes in Iraq were part of the mobilization plan. Terrorism had threatened the very core of the country's existence, and the war against terror was now a patriotic duty.

The news from the German election campaigns was received in the United States in a climate that left no room for nuances, fine distinctions or shades of gray. The only colors recognized were black and white. The Bush administration declared in consternation: "Schröder won the election on anti-Americanism." The reaction was swift and harsh. The word spread from the president's inner circle that Bush would never forget the disparaging gibes heard from Germany. He would never trust German Chancellor Gerhard Schröder again.

As for the pending dialogue on security policy, German voices were unwelcome. The Germans were in the doghouse. Many Americans stood behind their president. They had the feeling Bush had been subjected to a defamatory attack that came from Germany. The deceptive simplification was obvious: "The Germans compared us Americans with Hitler."

The Germans and French, who had anchored the anti-war coalition, bore the brunt of bitter recriminations against the European position on the Iraq war. All the rational, objective concerns about Bush's actions, which a great many Americans shared, barely registered. The surge of annoyance swept away the details of the Germans' concept for foreign policy.

But much more was at stake. Bush felt that the very core of his strategy had been challenged. The plan the White House and the Pentagon had in mind went far beyond what a single step against Iraq could signal. The reversal sought in Baghdad must be understood as an opening gambit, the first step toward achieving a democratic change of regime in Iran, Syria, Saudi Arabia and the other Arab nations. The plans envisioned an Islamic world with a democratic infrastructure, living in peace with Israel. In the Bush strategy, weapons would force the deep-seated cultural transformation in the Islamic world that unenlightened Islam had never achieved on its own.

Swift pursuit of this strategy undoubtedly required broad international support, and Bush saw Schröder and Chirac as standing squarely in the way. It was no secret in Washington that many nations shared the concerns of France and Germany. In U.S. domestic politics, blame for this distancing of the alliance partners was increasingly laid on the doorstep of the country's own government.

All of this explains the unusual magnitude of the damage done to transatlantic relations in the eyes of Washington. Europe has a communication problem that will be difficult to solve, and its strategic strength will be reassessed within that context. The wrath of the United States no longer accepts any alternative to answering the fundamental question of the logic and substance behind European foreign policy.

The relationship between Europe and the United States had already begun to deteriorate before September 11. Coolness, indifference and rivalry are the new parameters; accusations flying back and forth shape the conversation. September 11 and the events that followed strengthened this trend. In the current tense situation, the issue of Iraq more or less means escalation: Here too, each side apparently fails to understand the other. The Americans have largely ignored the fact that for most Europeans, the preferred solution to the Iraq issue—as well as to other crises—lies in diplomacy. And the Europeans fail to recognize that the United States sees its national security as threatened and intends to prevent another attack by any and all suitable means.

These different positions on transatlantic relations may have more serious effects on the Europeans than the Americans, for they have been shut out in retaliation despite their earnest wish to play a part in this concert of global powers. Meanwhile, the Americans are no longer willing to listen to accusations of unilateralism accompanied by one excuse after another for Europe's inability to forge 25 different opinions into a European defense policy.

European plans to establish a 60,000-man army that would occupy itself with the Petersberg tasks (humanitarian aid and rescue tasks, peacekeeping tasks as well as combat-force tasks in crisis management, including peacemaking) often are met in Washington with no more than sympathetic smiles. If Europe wants to be taken seriously as an international actor, it must begin the difficult process of negotiating increases in defense spending.

Public opinion in America on U.S. military action

Polls conducted by the Gallup Institute[28] after the 2004 election plainly showed that the majority of the U.S. population supported George W. Bush's clear stance in the fight against terrorism. His improved job performance rating opened the door to a second term in office. Domestic policy weaknesses or blunders and a growing mountain of debt played a secondary role when it came to guaranteeing the security of the American nation.

The American public springs to attention when its government takes military action. Examples include the 1986 bombing of Libya in retaliation for Libyan participation in the La Belle Discotheque bombing in Berlin, the 1993 missile attack on Iraq in response to the planned assassination of President Bush Sr. in Kuwait, the 1998 missile attacks on Afghanistan and the Sudan in retaliation for the U.S. embassy bombings in Kenya and Tanzania, and the wars against Afghanistan in 2001 and Iraq in 2003 with the declared objective of toppling regimes that support terrorism. Less publicized—though no less important—are the anti-terrorism measures put into place by

---

28 Cf. November 12, 2004, poll on overall job performance and Iraq in particular under www.gallup.com/poll/content/login.aspx?ci=14041 (accessed February 1, 2005).

banks, police, customs authorities and computer specialists, which serve to dry up terrorists' financial resources and constrain their everyday sphere of action.

However, the short-term military successes against the regimes in Afghanistan and Iraq should not be confused with conclusive success in the war on international terrorism. Regime change alone will not accomplish much. Consolidating peace and establishing economic prospects are necessary steps to deprive terrorism of its recruiting grounds over the long term. On that score, the process of nation building moves into the political foreground once again.[29]

The U.S. policy on fighting terror relies on four guiding principles: bringing terrorists to justice for their crimes; taking a hard-line approach with terrorists; exercising pressure on states and regimes that support terrorists; and finding and supporting allies in the fight against terror.[30] These principles are pursued with a variety of means and on a variety of levels, ranging from traditional diplomacy, international cooperation on economic sanctions, and secret missions all the way to military action.

But with short-term military actions standing in for a long-range plan for fighting terrorism, the United States is running the risk of being branded the aggressor and becoming the target of international criticism. This in turn could generate a rich crop of recruits for a new generation of terrorists.

Nevertheless, many Americans cannot or will not understand the depth and breadth of anti-Americanism in the Arabic world in particular. Although many in the United States call for a change in U.S. Middle East policy and for doubling the (significantly lower) development aid budget instead of increasing the defense budget as measures for fighting terrorism at its roots, these voices get drowned out in the everyday political noise of Washington.

Washington's verbal interaction with those states considered a political and military threat, where anti-Americanism is already smoldering, heats up resentment against the United States even further. Why should Cuba, Libya, Iran and North Korea—nations that the United States has publicly branded rogue states—look kindly on America?

---

29 Bertelsmann Stiftung 2005.

30 U.S. government report of June 2000: National Commission on Terrorism: Countering the Changing Threat of International Terrorism, Internet document: www.access.gpo.gov/nct (accessed February 1, 2005).

Because the very designation "rogue state" amounts to a verbal attack, former secretary of state Madeleine Albright sought to replace that term with the more moderate "state of concern." However, her effort was fruitless. The Bush administration returned to the stance that all rogue states deserved political and occasionally even military reprisals. What is more, it heightened the rhetoric by branding Iran, Iraq and North Korea as the "axis of evil." It soon expanded that term to include Cuba, Libya and Syria—indeed, any country accused of actively supporting terrorism and/or acquiring and distributing weapons of mass destruction. This political isolation of states not friendly to America has yet to show any signs of success.

Much of the American public still fails to recognize that exercising military power does not automatically lead to the desired objective. Proof positive is the widespread lack of understanding among Americans regarding the criticism or rebuff expressed by many European governments on the issue of the Iraq war. While Germany's war experience in particular is still based on World War II, and since then every military action has been subjected to harsh scrutiny, the loss in the Vietnam War by the United States—a superpower with a high percentage of its population uninformed on foreign policy—has only led to temporary critical self-reflection.[31]

However, after the attacks on the World Trade Center, the United States is facing challenges not only in the area of domestic security, but also with serious homegrown economic and social problems.

Domestic political challenges

Reactions to the terrorist threat—the need for homeland security

Bureaucratic reorganization to fight terror on the home front

The terror attacks of September 11, which radically altered U.S. foreign policy, also had broad repercussions for domestic policy. America considered the terrorist attacks not only an attack on the world

---

31 "USA: Die siegreiche Übermacht" by Klaus Larres, holder of the Kissinger Chair in Foreign Policy and International Relations at the Library of Congress in Washington DC, in: Handelsblatt, April 11/12, 2003, 8.

power's economic and military strength, but also an attack on the American way of life and the nation's fundamental values. Thus, the U.S. reaction necessarily involved more than a revamping of its foreign policy.

After the painful realization that U.S. territory is not invulnerable as had long been believed, and that the very elements of openness and mobility in American society had also served the terrorists' purposes, the government set out to reorganize homeland security in its entirety. The traditional chain of command for homeland security begins with the president, and continues down through the National Security Council to the relevant departments, particularly the Departments of State, Justice, Commerce and Treasury. Restructuring the domestic defense system meant overcoming the decades-old practice of separation between domestic law enforcement authorities and international intelligence agencies. For example, the CIA had always been prohibited from pursuing domestic intelligence activities—not just since its involvement in the Watergate affair, but since 1947.

To improve coordination in homeland defense and enable more efficient action, President Bush created a new agency for the "security of our homeland" in the first few weeks after September 11. The Office of Homeland Security was given comprehensive (though not particularly well-defined) powers with the objective of consolidating all anti-terror measures, and it was responsible for the entire coordination of homeland protection efforts.

Tom Ridge, until then governor of Pennsylvania, was named the first director of the Office of Homeland Security in October 2001. At the beginning of his tenure as homeland security director, there was a great deal of discussion about how his office figured into the defense structure; it was unclear whether he would report to the president or to Congress. Thus, while President Bush appointed Ridge to the office, there was no follow-up confirmation by Congress. This dispute was resolved in January 2003 by raising the status of the Office of Homeland Security to the level of a department (Department of Homeland Security). Accordingly, Ridge was sworn in on January 24, 2003, as the United States' first director of the Department of Homeland Security. Ridge was relieved by Michael Chertoff on March 3, 2005. Chertoff supervises approximately 180,000 government employees.[32]

---

32 Cf. Department of Homeland Security website: www.dhs.gov/dhs public/index.jsp.

Establishing a homeland security department constituted the most serious restructuring of the U.S. government since Harry S. Truman, similarly seeking to create a more effective defense structure, united the three branches of the military—the Air Force, the Navy and the Army—under the U.S. Department of Defense in 1947. Because the September 11 attacks made plain that security authorities could not guarantee domestic security, the 22 previously independent security agencies were placed under the control and coordination of the Department of Homeland Security. The department conducts joint security and threat analyses, monitors the security of borders, harbors and airports, and coordinates efforts for dealing with possible new crisis situations—all under the common goal of preventing further terrorist attacks.

Legislation and criminal prosecution

The bureaucratic reorganization also brought a toughening of laws. The terror attacks, though they struck hard, did not break down the structures of law and order to create a state of anarchy between the government and stateless terrorists. The United States remained a nation committed to the rule of law above all else.

There are a number of options for the criminal prosecution of international terrorists. The September 11 attacks could have been tried before an American court, as was done with the 1993 bombing of the World Trade Center; before a foreign court, as in the case of the Lockerbie trial, conducted in the Netherlands following Scottish law; or before an internationally recognized tribunal, such as the war crimes tribunals for Rwanda and the former Yugoslavia. In addition to criminal proceedings, civil suits could conceivably be filed by victims of the attacks or their next of kin and damages awarded from the frozen assets of the terrorists. The Bush administration, classifying the terrorists as unlawful combatants, chose to forgo the option of trying the defendants under international martial law.

An interesting feature of the domestic political reaction is that although President Bush announced a war on terrorism, Congress has never declared war. Thus, the United States is not officially at war, which would have granted the president far-reaching additional powers to the point of infringing on the Bill of Rights. And neither did Congress declare a state of national emergency, which also would have given the president special powers. Nevertheless, Congress did present the president with a resolution granting him a great deal of latitude, including the use of force to pursue those behind the September 11 attacks both at home and abroad and to prevent new attacks. In doing this, Congress cited article 1 section 8 of the U.S. Constitution, which allows Congress to "define and punish" offences against the law of nations by stateless actors—by military means, if necessary.[33]

Congress had to weigh the unlimited protection of human and civil rights guaranteed by the U.S. Constitution against the massive and comprehensive battle against terrorist threats. It gave the government additional instruments to take action against suspected terrorists. These included far-reaching options for surveillance and the opportunity to try foreign terrorists before a military court. But because this legislative development posed a striking contrast to the American tradition of human and civil rights, it was hounded by substantial protest and received the approval of Congress only after a time restriction was imposed on the new laws.

But, under pressure from the Bush administration, Congress also passed legislation in the name of fighting terrorism that allows justice authorities to indefinitely detain foreign citizens suspected of terrorism. In addition, options were expanded for intelligence agencies to use information collected about U.S. citizens or foreigners from criminal investigations for unlimited purposes. Congress also expanded opportunities for agencies to secretly search homes without notifying the subject of the search even after the fact.

At the same time, data protection has eroded even further. Not only can law enforcement agencies access and use confidential information about American and foreign students attending American universities, they have also been granted far greater powers for tapping private phone lines and Internet connections without solid suspicion. The new legislation left many questions about protection against abuse of authority unanswered, and the true constitutionality of these expanded powers will need to be clarified by the U.S. courts.

---

33 For more information, see Hongju Koh 2002, 138–161.

Public shock in the United States about September 11 and the ensuing political reaction in the areas of justice and law enforcement also led to a wave of patriotism and a sense of unity. Within a short time after the terror attacks, American flags were a scarce commodity in stores across the country, and flag manufacturers could barely keep up with demand. People united during their hour of need.

But as positive as this kind of patriotism can be, it can also have disastrous side effects. Critical scrutiny of the political process—the trademark of a democratic and plural society—have been branded as un-American and unpatriotic; insistence on fundamental rights hard-won over the last centuries has been viewed as aiding and abetting terrorists; musicians and artists who oppose terrorism but also speak out against the methods and actions of the U.S. government have been publicly criticized and their art banned.

At the beginning of the 21st century, the United States is threatening to revert to cultural McCarthyism and undermine the global eminence of its Bill of Rights with self-imposed censorship in the name of patriotism. Artists are already reminded of the National Socialist regime in Germany, where so-called degenerate art was banned and destroyed.[34] These domestic political consequences cannot simply be changed or controlled by legislative means. Only the American people can ensure that the values and fundamental beliefs that made their country what it is today will endure within its borders. It is up to the American people to uphold these values and beliefs regardless of the politics of the day.

Economic and social problems

At the beginning of the 21st century, the challenges facing the United States go beyond ensuring its own physical security. In addition to terrorist activities, economic and social issues threaten to test the stability of domestic security. What was just a whispered rumor in

---

34 American musician Marilyn Manson spoke out on this topic: "Ich bin Amerikas Alptraum." The rock musician Marilyn Manson, 33, on his Shock Art, creative self-censorship in the USA and his new CD. Der Spiegel 19 (2003), 178 f.

1988 had 10 years later become a shout: Significant segments of the American population have figured out that extremely serious domestic social and economic problems beset their country.

In a debate of unprecedented breadth in American history, the country began an internal dialogue as it approached the turn of the century—a dialogue that even on the surface contrasts strangely with the carefully celebrated restoration of American self-confidence vis-à-vis the outside world under Presidents Reagan and Bush.

In a nutshell, there are two distinct problem areas.

Economic problems—
from a creditor nation to the world's biggest debtor nation

On the list of domestic political priorities, right below the problem of domestic security comes concern about the economy. Within this complex web of issues, the widely fluctuating national debt—which has obviously become a permanent structural problem—towers over other topics.

By 1992, the United States had amassed the highest budget deficit in the nation's history under the presidency of George H. W. Bush—not least because of the 1991 Gulf War. The Reagan and Bush administrations had transformed the United States from a creditor nation into the world's largest debtor nation.[35] George H. W. Bush left the United States with an annual budget deficit of over $290 billion.

This handed incoming president Bill Clinton a total debt of over four trillion dollars. After lack of funding forced many government operations to shut down, the Clinton administration managed to wipe out the annual budget deficit with strict spending cuts. When Clinton left office in 2000, he actually left his successor George W. Bush with a budget surplus of $236 billion. However, the total national debt had risen above $5.5 trillion during Clinton's time in office.

After taking office, George W. Bush drove up government spending by increasing defense spending and introducing massive tax cuts. By 2002, the nation's annual budget deficit had climbed back to over $150 billion. After a record-setting year in 2004, in which the deficit

---

35 Cameron 2002, 15.

skyrocketed to over $412 billion, experts have projected a slight decline to $380 billion for 2005.[36] Every year the federal budget pays around $250 billion in interest on the U.S. national debt. This is approximately 11 percent of total annual spending by the American government.[37]

Exacerbating the problem of the budget deficit is the extremely low level of savings in the United States. Thus its deficit must be financed from foreign sources to a much greater degree than in Europe. The net debt currently amounts to 21.7 percent of America's gross domestic product.[38]

But the budget deficit is by no means the United States' only pressing economic problem. Due to the weak global economic situation, growth in GDP for 2001 slowed to 0.3 percent—compared to about 4 percent during the last three years of the Clinton administration—, the lowest level since 1991.[39] However, the United States seems to have already made it through the global economy's vale of tears. With a relative growth of 4.4 percent in GDP for 2004 and a projected 3.6 percent for 2005, the economy has once again been able to reach its prior performance levels. The enormous financial burden of the ongoing military operations in Afghanistan and Iraq stands in the way of higher growth levels.[40]

Nevertheless, many products are produced better and more cheaply abroad. And this in turn explains the now-chronic American trade deficit, which reached $668 billion in 2004—around six percent of GDP—and over the last five years grew by an average of 4.4 percent annually.[41]

Rounding out this picture is an insufficient investment rate, which for decades has only amounted to about half of that of Japan and is far below that of comparable industrialized nations. The average investment rate in the United States between 1950 and 1998 was 17.3 percent, while Germany's rate was 24.4 percent, France's 25.9 percent, and Japan even managed a rate of 29.4 percent.[42]

36 OECD Economic Outlook No. 77, Volume 2005/1 45–49.
37 Quoted from: United States Government Printing Office 2003, 369 ff.
38 OECD Economic Outlook No. 77, (loc. cit.).
39 United States Government Printing Office 2003, 274.
40 OECD Economic Outlook No. 77, (loc. cit.).
41 OECD 2002, 272 f.
42 "USA begrenzen Schulden im Ausland", appeared in Financial Times Deutschland, July 6, 2005, 16.

From an economic perspective, it is clear that the short-term high experienced under the Clinton administration did not fundamentally remedy structural economic problems such as the national debt, neglect of the infrastructure and insufficient savings and investment. Over recent decades, Americans have simply consumed too much, and beyond that have neglected to update their infrastructure and production facilities.

Social problems—the growing gap between rich and poor

Clearly linked to the state of the economy are shortcomings in social integration—though many Americans no longer take these as seriously as the economic problems.

Today, the American dream is out of reach for an increasing number of Americans. Around 33 million Americans—12 percent of the population—are considered poor according to official statistics. Two and a half million of the Americans living below the poverty level work full time.[43] The phenomenon of the working poor is a sad peculiarity of the social debate in the United States. Furthermore, approximately 41 million Americans—15 percent of the population—live without health insurance.[44]

Conditions in areas where the lower social classes live increasingly resemble those in developing countries, from basic socioeconomic data to everyday infrastructure. Although a general overview shows that open, even legally sanctioned discrimination against African-Americans and other minorities has almost entirely disappeared, social equality is still a long way off.

The increasingly obvious shortcomings in the education system pose an especially serious problem. These shortcomings in turn are a decisive cause for the increasing marginalization of large sections of the population. At its best, the American school system takes the lead worldwide. But a concentration on excellence at the top has led to an increasing neglect of education and job training for the broad masses. In the PISA study conducted by the OECD in 2000, the United States earned a mediocre ranking, significantly behind most Western indus-

---

43 See data from U.S. Census Bureau report on poverty: Proctor/Dalaker 2002.
44 Mills 2002, 3.

trialized nations. Over one in five students nationwide do not even graduate from high school.[45]

In view of the diverse challenges facing the United States, its prospects for the future must be questioned. Where is America headed?

Quo vadis, America?

Future prospects for a world power

In view of these findings, it is not surprising that many Americans see their country's position in the world as threatened. To be sure, a vocal segment of the American public decries any debate about an American crisis as the talk of defeatist liberals. Hailing back to President Franklin D. Roosevelt's famous line "The only thing we have to fear is fear itself," those in this camp view the warning that America faces a decline as the real danger. While they acknowledge the need to remedy shortcomings here or there, they deny that the issues to be tackled differ in quality from the challenges of past eras.

At the other end of the opinion spectrum are the declinists, who adhere to the theory popularized by Paul M. Kennedy: The United States, like other world powers before it, is doomed to an inevitable decline; sociopolitical measures can only cushion the fall.[46]

According to the declinists, the United States has overstretched its economic capacity through its involvement overseas, primarily by its global military presence, but also by the transfer of resources such as development and economic aid. This has squandered the nation's means for rebuilding its economic strength. As a consequence, military spending and foreign aid payments must be drastically reduced.

However, this theory does not adequately explain the current situation. Even the empirical data fail to support it. In spite of its substantial investment in arms technology during the Cold War as well as after September 11, the United States has never spent more than six percent of its GDP on the military.[47] Thus, military spending can-

---

45 See U.S. Census Bureau data on education levels: www.census.gov/population/soc-demo/education/ppl-169/tab01.txt (accessed February 1, 2005).

46 Kennedy 2000, 758–787.

47 United States Government Printing Office 2003, 276, 300.

not be blamed for the economic decay of the United States so vividly predicted by declinists.

As for development aid, the United States in fact trails most Western states: U.S. spending comes in at 0.13 percent, while Germany spends 0.37 percent of its gross domestic product on development aid.[48]

Most of the American academic community has roundly criticized Kennedy's ideas. But the theories are still relevant as a portrait of a certain political sensitivity; they encapsulate concepts widely held—though often vaguely enunciated—by the American public. In the same vein are calls for trade restrictions against supposedly cheating trade partners. The Americans—no less than other nationalities—can be tempted to blame their problems on other countries. Declinism meets this need for a scapegoat.

Declinist theory is particularly dangerous because of the way it misrepresents the nature of foreign relations. A pet refrain of the declinists is that the cost of U.S. involvement abroad outweighs the advantages it has brought. This attitude does much to explain the public tendency to view expenditures on foreign and international policy solely as a drain on resources. By the same token, the American public tends to regard its own foreign policy as primarily carrying out moral obligations.

American perceptions of social deficits in the United States

Granted its premises, this notion makes a certain amount of sense. If foreign policy does not depend on functional, interest-based—in other words, selfish—calculations, then it must be framed as looking after foreign interests. Thus, the American presence in Europe becomes an altruistic act, the strong helping the weak. As many a visitor to the United States can confirm, attempts to suggest to the Americans that this presence in fact serves their own interests often fall on deaf ears.

---

48 Data on public development cooperation from the Federal Ministry for Economic Cooperation and Development: www.bmz.de/infothek/hintergrundmaterial/statistiken/stat_08b1.pdf.

Those who would attribute domestic problems to foreign policy ramifications fail to consider the facts at hand—but that is not all. Even if they were right, America cannot shut itself off as an island of the blessed. In a shrinking world that is increasingly interconnected, where everything is everybody's business, the United States—like every other country—is an integral part of the global economy.

Nothing demonstrates this more clearly than America's double deficit (trade and budget deficit). The threat posed by many other developments pales in comparison. Even the United States must bow to the economic law of comparative cost. If many goods can be produced better and more cheaply elsewhere, this also boosts prosperity at home—provided that the United States pays for such goods with exports of its own, not with credit. So the best approach would be to further embrace the global market, not shut it out.

Furthermore, the declinist critique also lacks a sense of proportion. It cannot be denied, for example, that the American share of global gross national product—a favorite statistic cited by declinists—has slipped significantly since the end of World War II. In 1946, it stood at 45 percent; by 2002 it had dropped to 21.4 percent. But this can easily be explained in terms of the obviously unusual circumstances of the time: All economic powers of any importance, apart from the United States, had suffered severe—even devastating—destruction in the war. Since the world's recovery from the impact of war, the U.S. share of global GNP has hovered consistently around 22 to 23 percent.

Nor is it enough to look at economic criteria alone. Not only is the United States indisputably the world's leading military state—and set to remain so for the foreseeable future—, it is also (notwithstanding any European smugness on this point) a first-class cultural power. As but one indication of its prominence in this arena, the United States clearly dominates the film industry—undoubtedly the premier artistic medium of the 20th and 21st centuries.

All this is enough to demonstrate that America's lead remains secure for the foreseeable future—though that time horizon is steadily shrinking. In the worst-case scenario, the U.S. lead over its rivals might dwindle. Europe may catch up, but it will never move ahead.

To recognize this is not to deny that the United States faces pressing problems. However, it is becoming clear that these difficulties do not demand more than the sort of routine measures any government must take to adapt to new developments. This does not mean that if the United States simply gives American virtues free rein, everything will be fixed. Indeed, the very intransigence of the current situation seems to be rooted in the fact that the traditional problem-solving techniques afforded by America's political culture are inadequate to deal with its crises.

Causes for the growing social discrepancy

Particularly in the area of social policy, one obvious and significant source of difficulty is quite simply the unwillingness of American taxpayers to pay for these programs. The income and sales tax burden for the average American lies at a mere 27 percent, compared to about 34 percent in Great Britain, 51 percent in France and 46 percent in Germany.[49]

This reveals a crucial problem. Historically, the United States is the "liberal" country—in the classic sense of the word—born of a tax rebellion (think of the Boston Tea Party), and defined from the very outset as an effort to keep broad segments of citizens' lives free from state control. The underlying assumption is that citizens can solve their problems better than the government. In contrast, conservatism and social democracy—the two most important political movements in Europe—require a strong government, albeit for different reasons.

However, the call for government intervention to address urgent economic and social problems has been sounded repeatedly over the years in the United States as well. President Clinton's failed effort to reform the health sector, social security, education and job training was the first direct attempt to address these problem areas with comprehensive action by the state. Its conceptual underpinning lay in the realization that providing a high-quality education for everyone is by far the most important cornerstone of a thriving economy. President George W. Bush has also attempted—so far without success—to reform the educational system by distributing school vouchers paid for with tax dollars for students to attend private schools.

But the American public still balks at supporting the government intervention such plans entail. Therein lies the reason for the continued failure of these attempts.

49 Carey/Tchilinguirian 2000.

The Republican majority in Congress is once again advocating the view that cuts in assistance for the socially disadvantaged will strengthen their initiative and could lead them out of poverty. For this reason, a reduction in social benefits—along with tax cuts for the average citizen—are recommended on a broad front. However, evidence that this approach can actually lead the poorer segments of society out of poverty is not yet forthcoming. This expectation appears even more illusory because the job training and certification programs that would be necessary for success do not fit in with the concept of a business environment free of state involvement.

It is very clear that the Bill of Rights is viewed solely as protection from the government for citizens. In sharp contrast to the European perspective, the United States lacks the social dimension of its fundamental rights. In Europe, guaranteeing fundamental social rights is considered a responsibility of the state—both according to Christian social teachings and from the standpoints of socialism and social democracy.

If the bedrock of America's stance—its belief in the power of individuals to solve their problems free from interference by the government—cannot support the task of overcoming current critical problems, it makes sense to recommend that the United States look abroad—and specifically to European experience. Although it is true that social welfare costs have placed a heavy burden on Europe's state budgets, social program expenditures have thus far spared Europe the kinds of sociopolitical conflicts found in many American cities and suburbs.

It would be naive and unrealistic to advise the Americans to simply emulate European strategies. In an increasingly interdependent world, however, a degree of cross-fertilization in strategic approaches would certainly bear fruit, ultimately reducing social costs for both sides. Indeed, Europe could learn a great deal from the United States in many areas, including fostering academic excellence, improving the university system and dealing with the dynamics of social change in general. Structuring this exchange as a learning community would be beneficial for both sides.[50]

---

50 Bertelsmann Stiftung et. al. 2000.

New ethnic composition of the United States

Will Europe and the European heritage continue to play the same role in the United States in the future as it does now? Data from the U.S. census taken in 2000 painted an impressive portrait of the most recent demographic development in the United States. According to current statistics from 2002, of the 281.4 million people living in America, 11.9 million were born as foreign citizens.[51]

Ethnic displacement and its consequences

Of this group of people, according to the 2002 data, only 20 percent originally came from Europe. In 1970, the percentage of U.S. citizens born in Europe was still 62 percent. By contrast, the percentage of U.S. citizens born in Asia climbed between 1970 and 2002 from nine to 33 percent. During the same period, the percentage of Latin Americans rose from 19 to 38 percent.[52] However, by far the greatest percentage of naturalized U.S. citizens comes from Central America (including Mexico), comprising two-thirds of the foreign population.[53] Almost 20 million—including foreign persons born in the United States—reported speaking a language other than English at home. Of those, 10.7 million spoke Spanish and 2.7 million spoke an Asian language.[54]

No doubt about it: The United States is a dynamic magnet for immigration. Approximately 400,000 people flow into the United States every year as legal immigrants. This trend will continue for the time being.[55] California—America's most populated state, with 34.5 million residents—is particularly affected by immigration (along with

51 U.S. Census Bureau: Current Population Survey, March 2002, Internet Release Date: March 10, 2003, www.census.gov/population/socdemo/foreign/ppl-162/ tab01-01.pdf (accessed February 1, 2005).
52 U.S. Census Bureau: Foreign-Born Population by World Region of Birth, Citizenship and Year of Entry: March 2002, www.census.gov/population/socdemo/foreign/ppl-162/tab02-01.pdf (accessed February 1, 2005).
53 U.S. Census Bureau: Population Profile of the United States: 2000 (Internet Release), www.census.gov/population/pop-profile/2000/chap17.pdf (accessed February 1, 2005).
54 U.S. Census Bureau: P20. Household Language by Linguistic Isolation, 2000, http:// factfinder.census.gov/servlet/DTTable?_ts=75710191010 (accessed February 1, 2005).
55 U.S. Department of Justice. Immigration and Naturalization Service: Annual Report. Legal Immigration, Fiscal Year 2001, Number 7, August 2002, 5–8.

New York, Florida and Texas). Caucasian Americans of European descent are already in the minority there, accounting for just 46.7 percent of the population in 2000; nationwide the percentage is still 69.1 percent. The percentage of the population with Hispanic heritage is 32.5 percent in California, while the percentage of Hispanics in the United States overall is 12.5 percent.[56]

Clearly, the vast majority of new immigrants are not of European origin. So should we expect the United States to become a different country, culturally speaking? Is Europe at risk of sinking below the American horizon as the ties of European heritage fade into the minority?

Even those who accept the American way of life more or less without reservation often retain a certain fondness for their homeland. Though it may be just sentimental attachment, it can occasionally affect their actions. So it stands to reason that people whose American identity embraces their roots would want the United States to take into account, in one way or another, the foreign policy interests of their country of origin. There are impressive examples of this throughout American history. The most significant of these is the remarkable influence of the Jewish population, which has steadily worked to ensure close ties with Israel, the new-old homeland, since the Six-Day War.

But just as striking are those examples showing the opposite, particularly that of Americans with German heritage. These form the largest of the identifiable ethnic minorities but have never managed to exert any real influence on American foreign policy.

The rise of East Asia—which is currently limited to the region's economic growth—is undoubtedly a development of utmost significance that demands the attention of the United States and every other nation with global interests. This, rather than the rising wave of Asian immigrants, explains heightened U.S. involvement in developments in the region.

People who immigrate to the United States do so because of the country's appeal—because the United States as it is seems preferable to the social realities of their country of origin. At the same time, it is

---

56 Data for the year 2000. U.S. Census Bureau: State and County Quick Facts. California, http://quickfacts.census.gov/qfd/states/06000.html (accessed February 1, 2005).

natural to expect that people might draw on their experiences in their home country to work for change in the United States.

Also worth noting, however, is that the current ethnic displacement in the United States is taking place against the backdrop of a sometimes quite passionate debate on America's real or imagined eurocentrism. The objective demographic changes seem to be followed in astonishingly short order by a corresponding shift in American identity.

European models on the retreat

Those who criticize American eurocentrism claim that American identity is based far too much on European models, that historical interpretations are always viewed from the European perspective and that contributions to building the nation by Americans not of European descent have been ignored.

Consequently, the eurocentrism debate goes hand in hand with historical revisionism on a broad scale. The substantial cultural implications were particularly evident during the 500th anniversary year of Columbus' discovery. For centuries, the European conquest of America as begun by Columbus was celebrated as part of the inexorable advance of progress. As a result, the native inhabitants fell victim to an attitude inspired by Social Darwinism and were dismissed as history's losers. Now the eurocentrism debate has opened the door to a diametrically opposed interpretation.

America's pre-Columbian culture has increasingly been associated with one attribute after another of utopian perfection. This development reached its peak with Kirkpatrick Sale's *The Conquest of Paradise*. The author expressly applies the concept of paradise not only as a metaphor, but also as a literal description of the native inhabitants' way of life at the time of the Europeans' arrival.[57] For a Europe deeply mired in crisis since the end of the Middle Ages, America offered a chance to heal itself. Instead, driven by primitive material greed, the Europeans destroyed that way of life, according to Sale. This interpretation brings us back to Rousseau's concept of the noble savage. America became the white man's fall from grace. At the same time,

57 Sale 1990.

we come full circle to our intellectual starting point: One ethnocentric approach, albeit a non-European one, has replaced the other.

The practical and tangible consequences of this trend first surfaced in education policy. Respected American universities as well as the state bodies responsible for curriculum planning have begun to examine the traditional educational canons. European history and literature are being edged out in favor of the history and cultures of countries to the south.

From Europe's perspective, this is nothing less than an attempt to eradicate, or at least weaken, America's European roots. And yet, to claim that this development is aimed against Europe would be to miss the point.

To elucidate this, we must look at the eurocentrism debate in a broader historical context. The patriotism that sustained the American people during the bitter struggle for survival that won their independence from the English colonialists in the 18th century was a constitutional patriotism. The United States wanted to be different from the old Europe.

But another fact is equally important: From the beginning of its aspirations as a nation, this selfsame America considered itself firmly English in culture—and indeed, its population was overwhelmingly English. True, the United States never was a nation state after the European model. But the American identity—certainly comparable in this regard to the nations of Europe—was nonetheless essentially rooted in a sense of belonging to a homogeneous nation defined by objective characteristics such as language, heritage, religion and customs.

Thus, the identity of the United States contained an element of ambivalence from the start. The strong expectation of unity established during the Revolution did fade at first. But as huge waves of immigrants from other European countries—notably Ireland and Germany—rolled in during the first half of the 19th century, they encountered a significant amount of resistance on the grounds that such un-English immigrants would not be capable of integration.

The other possible approach to shaping an identity—that is, the attempt to define being an American subjectively and normatively through shared values and beliefs—was for long periods of American history applied only half-heartedly. The liberation of slaves, born of this spirit of normative challenge, slowed to a halt after the American

Civil War. Up until the civil rights movement of the 1950s, African-Americans were fobbed off with the phrase "separate but equal," which in reality meant "separate and unequal." This, too, expressed an attempt to preserve an ethnic identity.

Two developments during the 20th century gradually led Americans away from their ethnic identity once more. On the one hand, World War I required them to hark back to the values on which their nation was founded. How otherwise to justify a war against the Germans, who by now comprised a large percentage of the American population? Furthermore, the confrontation with the totalitarian National Socialist and communist regimes made it imperative to define and fortify a conceptual counterweight.

On the other hand, a new wave of immigration washed over the United States just before the turn of the century—this time from Italy, Austro-Hungary and Russia. The ethnic identity once defined by western Europeans now included the whole of Europe. The universalist tendency inherent in human rights was reflected in the universalization of the nation's ethnic composition. Viewed in this light, the mass immigration from non-European countries is merely the next logical step in this development. The United States has truly become the nation of nations, transcending any idea of ethnic identity.

New normative frames of reference for the American social order

For the United States, it is now a matter of avoiding the dangers of cultural particularism. A society based on a rigorous application of human rights must, logically, enable each group to claim its own cultural contributions and achievements. However, this can only be successful if the framework defined by these human rights is acknowledged as a common point of reference.

Otherwise, groups defined by ethnicity or other factors such as religion or gender are left to jostle among themselves without the possibility for arbitration, without a higher system of norms for regulating conflict. This would have dissolved not only any ethnic identity, but any national identity at all, seriously threatening the continued existence of the United States as a coherent community.

But the idea of human rights as a normative frame of reference is undoubtedly of European origin. Therefore, the non-European minorities must resist the temptation to reject or relativize this frame of reference. Conversely, representatives of the mainstream—that is, the members of society with European leanings in both a philosophical and ethnic sense—must be prepared not to resist further cultural universalization.

The United States today is confronted by serious crises in a number of social areas. For the first time in the nation's history, its confidence that it stands as a role model for the world has been thoroughly shaken. This has led many to fear the end of "America, the chosen land." But the real historical task of the United States remains intact. The United States is and will remain the experimental ground for building and shaping a truly universal society.

4 The European Union on the path to political completion

The development of the original European Economic Community (EEC) with its six founding member states to form today's European Union with 25 member states reads like a success story. Yet the integration process was difficult and fraught with setbacks. This chapter describes the foreign policy challenges facing the European Union, in particular the step-by-step development of its foreign and security policy capacities after the end of the Cold War. It highlights the challenges to Europe's stability and domestic policy inherent in its enlargement and integration, and ends with an overview of how the Americans view Europe's increasing unity.

Europe at the beginning of the 21st century

Historic opportunity to unite the Continent

The European Union is striving toward completion. Despite many positive and successful integration efforts, the rejection of the EU Constitution by France and the Netherlands has cast a dark shadow over the goal of finality. With the introduction of the euro into circulation on January 1st, 2002, the national currency borders fell in the first 12 member states, and the Economic and Monetary Union has put a tangible face on European identity. EU enlargement presents a historic opportunity, opening up the possibility of a pan-European union. The integration will first cross the borders of Latin Europe, then Christian Europe. For this reason, the European Union needs to determine the extent and intensity of its integration and define its role in the world.

At the beginning of the 21st century, the European Union must deal with the consequences of the most extensive enlargement in its history. The December 2002 decision made by the European Council in Copenhagen added 10 new members from Central and Eastern Europe as well as Cyprus and Malta, effective May 1, 2004.[58]

However, even this enlarged European Union has not completed the territorial and political unification of Europe. With the decision by the heads of state and government to open accession negotiations in October 2005, Turkish membership became just as much of a possibility as the integration of Southeastern Europe. Negotiations were also opened on this date with Croatia, albeit with the caveat that its government must fully cooperate with the Hague tribunal for war crimes in the former Yugoslavia. On February 9, 2006 the European Commission entered officially into detailed accession talks with both Croatia and Turkey.[59]

Step-by-step integration toward the "United States of Europe"

Several concurrent processes will shape the face of Europe over the next few years. With regard to foreign policy, the European Union will need to shoulder more responsibility in its own backyard. The Treaty establishing a Constitution for Europe outlined the institutional and procedural framework necessary for effective action. Should the Constitution or parts of it enter into force, Europe's leaders must then make use of that framework to formulate policies with a strategic fundament—not mere declarations, but plans that can be vigorously implemented.[60] The pragmatic deepening of integration in the tiniest of steps—a community approach that often still relies on the principle of unanimity—has reached its limits. Further steps toward loosening national sovereignties are necessary, but they require a more precise definition of the scope and goal of European unification.

With the broadening and deepening of the integration process, questions about common concepts and definitions of European identity, solidarity and stability have been pushed to center stage. The final keystone in the arch of integration must be set over the next 10 years.

58 Copenhagen European Council, Presidency Conclusions, December 12/13, 2002, EU document SN 400/02
59 "Accession talks proper all set to start for Croatia and Turkey," 8 February, 2006, www.euractive.com (accessed February 14, 2006)
60 Weidenfeld 2005a.

Like the United States, Europe is going through a profound change in its self-image and structure, with the outcome still unclear. For Europe, even more than for the United States, this is a consequence of the drastic structural upheaval that followed the collapse of the Soviet Union. Since the end of the East-West conflict, the systemic change associated with integration has quickened its pace. Contradictory tendencies toward integration and disintegration have played out simultaneously; supranational politics have woven a closer web at the same time that formerly coherent nations and regions fanned out into diversity.[61]

The extent of supranational integration is greater now than at any other time during the last 50 years, and yet the idea of Europe, the concept of a future together, has never been more scattered and publicly disputed. Nevertheless, Europe in its current form offers a wealth of opportunity unparalleled in history. Several concurrent projects symbolize the dynamic for the integration and the cohesion of its members: progress toward territorial unity in Europe; ongoing development in the security and defense sector, made all the more necessary by September 11 and the U.S.-dominated wars in Afghanistan and Iraq; the process introduced in Lisbon in March 2000 on building a modern information society[62] and efforts to establish a region of freedom, security and justice.

These projects give concrete expression to the vague images of completing the integration process. The fight against international terrorism notwithstanding, Europe's political unity will arise less from concrete resistance to external threats than from the shared market and the steady definition and widening of the European model for solidarity and society in a global marketplace—and all this before a backdrop of completed and anticipated rounds of enlargement. Europe's territorial reach is not based on imperialism; its borders will emerge through voluntary normative consensus among current and future member states.

---

61 For global political development trends after the end of the East-West conflict, see Link 2001.

62 Lisbon European Council, Presidency Conclusions, March 23/24, 2000, http://ue. eu.int/newsroom/LoadDoc.asp?MAX=1&BID=76&DID=60941&LANG=4 (accessed February 1, 2005), which formulates a strategy for the EU to realize the most competitive world market power possible.

However, the accelerated pace of integration prompts a vastly increased skepticism and reserve at the national level.[63] In general, the importance of national and regional accession to Europe is rising. Within the European Union, an unmistakable trend toward renationalization has taken the form of a partial return to classical models of power. This can be seen not only in some member states' stubborn insistence on protecting national sovereignty, but also in their foreign policy. The fissure within the EU between backers and opponents of the war in Iraq made very clear that most member states focus primarily on internal politics; the broad European perspective comes in second.

In a parallel development, economic and political situations—and especially their problems—increasingly have international repercussions. But the development of appropriate political decision-making structures at the European level has lagged behind, making it impossible to relieve pressures that the individual states cannot handle. Europe is in a bind. The magnet of integration is attracting more and more politicians and countries keen to accede to the EU—but its capacity for action at a supranational level cannot keep pace. The Continent is in danger of becoming a victim of its own success.

These simultaneous and opposing developments define the singular profile of Europe today. Surrounded by uncertain constellations, beset with new conflicts, pulled and pushed by unmet demands, the Europeans are struggling to get their bearings straight. The United States is challenging this complicated Europe to define its interests clearly—and expects it to have instruments in place to pursue those interests. Thus, any realignment of the transatlantic partnership will require the Europeans to do their basic homework—with development of a global security policy heading the list.

In the midst of its own identity crisis, Europe will not abandon the image of America built up over the decades. America's contribution to the reconstruction of Europe and to the joint defense of freedom against Communism has become a fixture in European identity. Even as it concentrates more intently on its own internal development, Europe will maintain its ties to the United States. America, its

---

63 Weidenfeld/Wessels 2004.

first partner, will remain the natural partner both for resolving issues within Europe and for responding to global challenges.

At the same time, Europeans must confront on their own the challenges that come with advancing integration and enlargement. To evaluate their chances for success, it is worth taking a look at how the EU has reacted to radical changes in the political framework in Europe and around the world since the end of the East-West conflict.

Setting a course toward effective foreign policy action

Changing constellations after the end of the Cold War

The end of the East-West conflict has resulted in obvious shifts on the political map of Europe. Old allegiances, losing their importance, have been replaced by new political force fields. And over the long term, foreign policy orientations will adjust to the changes accordingly. The new alignments on the Continent are clear: France has shifted from the center of Western Europe to a position on the margins of the Continent—all the more so as democracy and market economy gain a foothold beyond Germany's eastern borders.

Prior to 1989, Europe did not have a center of any political relevance and therefore avoided the problems of allegiance related to a central position. Since then, old concepts have been revised: Germany now sees itself, albeit under different conditions, as part of the West yet situated between East and West. Austria is confronted with new, unprecedented claims, expectations and opportunities to exert influence on its flanks. Even Italy cannot turn a blind eye to the conflict in the Balkans—the Adriatic is both barrier and bridge. New zones are emerging within Europe:
- Southern Europe, previously the poorer member states of the European Union, whose material expectations are seen as competing with the East for resources;
- that part of Western Europe containing the two nuclear powers France and Great Britain, whose nuclear influence and political roles are declining;
- the western part of Central Europe with Germany and Austria, which—despite their geographical position in the West—are most directly affected by developments in Eastern Europe;

- the Adriatic region with Italy, which is most strongly influenced by the upheavals in Southeastern Europe;
- Northern Europe, which has lost its significance as a partially neutral area providing a gentle transition from West to East;
- Eastern Europe around the European part of Russia, whose future will be influenced by its political distance from and geographical proximity to Russia;
- Southeastern Europe, whose separation from West and East Central Europe has resulted from the ethnic conflicts of the 1990s and the still latent political ambitions of the key states in the region, and which is just now finally moving toward military and political ties with the West.

All these regions lack homogeneous organizational structures. Still, these locational differences explain differences in national and integrationist strategies. They are the backdrop for interest in deepening or enlarging the European Union; they are the source of national concepts of integration, control and distribution of resources within the European Community.

At the same time, world history rolls on, and Europe cannot withdraw from global politics to deal with its own problems undisturbed. With its attacks on the Western democratic world, international terrorism challenged not only the United States, but Europe as well. As the recent horrific attacks on Madrid in March 2004 and London in July 2005 made clear, terror has arrived on the old continent as well. International terrorism is forcing Europe to undertake an unprecedented level of global action. The engagement of European states in Afghanistan and Iraq was just a harbinger of a development that will have far-reaching implications within the sphere of the war on terror and will demand comprehensive action on multiple levels from the Europeans.

The European Union must ensure the security of its members and citizens at home and abroad. This is an essential fundament of the European Community. The common foreign and security policy must be developed further to ensure Europe's ability to act effectively—instead of offering daily fodder for political caricatures. Existing security organizations must be realigned to suit the changed realities. This includes establishing a collective security system that incorporates American as well as European interests equally.

Improving stability by enlarging the Union

Greater diversity and new neighbors

The European Union is entering a new era not only with regard to its internal configuration, but also in terms of its international engagement and its geographic expanse. Enlargement is creating new neighborhoods and a region of increasing diversity. The EU's expansion to 25 members—and possibly even 27 before too long—is drawing new borders for the Union, from the Barents Sea in the distant north to the Black Sea in the southeast. The possible accession of Turkey even opens up the Caucasus and Middle East as geostrategic neighbors. All of the activities, conflicts and different development levels spanning the borders in and around these regions will become topics for European policy. Thus, the European Union finds itself in an exposed position, with deep-seated changes and upheavals pressing in on all sides.

The first round of enlargement in 2004 had already pushed the European Community to the borders of the Russian Federation, Ukraine, Belarus and the Republic of Moldova. Surrounded by Poland and Lithuania, the Kaliningrad region belonging to Russia has created a Russian enclave within the European Union. Europe has new neighbors that are politically unstable, ethnically polarized and economically shaky. Topping that list is the Russian Federation, whose political system demonstrates both a strong state system and weak crisis management and whose economic order profits from climbing oil and gas prices in the world market over the medium term but shows minimal progress on structural reform and increasing investments. Even after the end of the East-West conflict, substantial asymmetries continue to exist between the European Union and the Russian Federation, posing a risk to stability and security all across Europe.[64]

In the case of Ukraine and the Republic of Moldova, the European Union is faced with significant discrepancies between these countries' desire to join the EU and their ongoing transition problems. Due to their persistent political instability, economic crises and weak civil societies, these neighboring states constitute a security risk that

---

64 Cf. Kempe 2000.

so far has received too little attention. At the same time, current EU policy also runs the risk of excluding its neighbors to the east by drawing new dividing lines to ensure stability in Europe.[65]

One step in the right direction is the new European Neighborhood Policy, a forward-looking strategy crafted by Günter Verheugen as EU commissioner for enlargement. In essence, it states that stability and prosperity within the European Union are closely linked with the new neighbor states bordering the enlarged EU. To move this concept ahead, the EU established a Wider Europe Task Force to flesh out the new policy area with concrete initiatives. Since its inception, the task force has drafted action plans for the countries and regions concerned, that is, in Eastern Europe and the southern Mediterranean region.[66]

The decision of December 17/18, 2004, to open accession negotiations with Turkey in October 2005 has similarly far-reaching implications.[67] Doubts about EU membership for that nation were met with the argument that Europe is not bound to the Christian religion. This complies with the Union's view of itself as an open, plural, and ideologically neutral entity. But that argument has a logical extension. If cultural identity falls away as a criterion, there is no reason to reject the eventual accession of other states—the Russian Federation, Ukraine, the Republic of Moldova, the Caucasus republics, the states of the Middle East and North Africa.[68]

However, the category of identity could be replaced by the logic of stability. Since the end of political bipolarity, the anarchic platform of international politics has been seeking new models of order. Globalization is stealing from politics in general the power to shape events and circumstances. Therefore, a new, wider region of European stability could become just as significant as a North America extending clear down to South America or an Asiatic region led by China and Japan in tandem.

65 Kempe 2001.
66 Conference of the European Council in Thessaloniki, June 19–20, 2003, Presidency Conclusions, Chapter V, under: http://ue.eu.int/ueDocs/cms_Data/docs/press-Data/de/ec/76285.pdf (accessed January 13, 2005).
67 Conference of the European Council in Brussels, December 17–18, 2004, Presidency Conclusions, under http://ue.eu.int/ueDocs/cms_Data/docs/pressDa ta/de/ec/83221.pdf (accessed January 13, 2005).
68 On the question of who belongs to Europe, see among others Weidenfeld 1997a, 297–303 and 1985.

Furthermore, an enlarged European Union with Turkey as a member would have direct borders with Syria, Iraq, Iran, Armenia and Georgia. This prospect entails its own risks and poses a major challenge to stability policy. To the northeast of Turkey, for example, the EU would share a border with Armenia and Georgia—two countries that (at least in the case of Armenia) have unfriendly relations with Turkey and as former republics of the Soviet Union fall directly within the Russian Federation's sphere of influence.

Adding to this risk landscape (now increasingly relevant to the European Union and its European neighborhood policy) is the Balkan region, which the Union would have girdled. Developments in the former Yugoslavia have shown that the European Union can successfully promote and consolidate democracy and security in the Balkans by providing political and economic incentives. The June 2003 resolution of the European Council of Thessaloniki to offer the countries of the western Balkans concrete prospects for accession to the European Union must also be viewed against this backdrop.

The success or failure of its European neighborhood initiatives will have direct repercussions for Europe on many fronts: trade networks and channels for raw materials, armaments and weapons proliferation, transnational crime, fundamentalist movements, migration trends and environmental threats. Therefore, in addition to managing internal conflicts with minority groups, the European Union's security policy will concentrate heavily on this aspect of international relations.[69]

The prospect of a large new zone of stability has its own merits. A European Union with 28 member states (EU–28) would surpass the United States in population, territorial area and economic strength. Its potential would equal that of a world power, accounting for one-third of global production and world trade. However, an EU–28 would also feature enormous economic diversity, so that it might be occupied first and foremost with internal conflicts.

But can Europe develop a strategic plan for stability in the neighborhood and use its resources to implement it? Without a deeper cultural

---

69 On the issue of institutional framework options for the European Union, see Czempiel 1999.

understanding among Europeans of their history, confrontations and interests, it will be impossible to draft an effective European neighborhood strategy. A vital benchmark for European integration will be the degree to which independent cultures can exist side by side.[70]

In view of this neighborhood panorama, Europe must develop a capacity for action of an entirely new quality. Changing borders and new fields of action are bringing greater pressure toward integration in the area of common foreign, security and defense policy. The European Union will take on the role of a crisis management system for collective security. In this way, the European Union will act as an anchor for security policy alongside the European Community as an economic power.[71]

The EU as a defense alliance

Baby steps toward a common European defense policy

The European Security and Defense Policy (ESDP) is a chapter of European integration that not only goes back several decades, but also has seen more ups and downs than any other policy area.

After World War II, the countries of Europe were interested primarily in a European structure that would ensure peace in Europe over the long term. The means to this end would be an integration policy to create a supranational control system by relinquishing national sovereignty in key areas, thus rendering warlike aggression by individual countries impossible. Pooling the war resources of coal and steel under the European Coal and Steel Community (ECSC) in 1951 was the first step in this direction.

The 1954 attempt to establish a European Defense Community (EDC) envisaged a collective defense system for member states of the ESCS. A parallel effort set out to institutionalize the European Political Community (EPC), although that would have required transferring significant aspects of national sovereignty to the Community level. The threat of Communism and confrontation between East and West inspired these plans, whose authors intended to emphasize

---

70 Wessels 1995, 486–496.
71 See among others: 1999 International Bertelsmann Forum

Europe's independence between the two blocs. But fears of Germany regaining political and military strength scuttled these plans with a veto in the French parliament. Instead, NATO developed into the guarantor of security for the Western world. The Western European Union (WEU) founded in 1954 offered no substitute for the EDC plans, for NATO overshadowed the WEU right from the start.

With the accession of the militarily neutral states of Ireland and Denmark in 1973, the European Communities took a further step away from a being a defense community. The policy of détente pursued by both superpowers in the 1970s in the Conference on Security and Cooperation in Europe (CSCE) did its part to encourage the belief that an independent defense community was not an urgent necessity.

In the 1980s, as a more strident tone returned to relations between the superpowers and a new arms race took off, the European threat analysis changed. Concerns also mounted that Europe would be caught between the millstones of the superpowers' interests.

Not until 1987, with the Single European Act (SEA), did a foundational treaty formalize the instrument of European Political Cooperation (EPC) initiated in 1970 as a mechanism for decision-making and coordination outside the bounds of the Community treaties. But the security and defense policy aspects were excluded; as a result, the European Communities remained exclusively dependent on the collective defense system of NATO. Although the WEU was upgraded institutionally, it still clearly remained in the shadow of NATO. Thus, right up to the end of the East-West conflict, national sovereignty reservations and Alliance interests dominated every approach to drafting a supranational defense system, effectively blocking any chance for substantial progress.

Europe's architecture for peace after the East-West conflict

Only the collapse of the Soviet Union, bringing the end of the East-West conflict and changes in the global security policy milieu, has allowed the European Communities to detach themselves somewhat from American protection and begin serious efforts toward an independent security and defense policy. At the same time, the instability of the former Soviet republics in Eastern Europe has made the need for a European peace architecture obvious.

In the Maastricht Treaty of 1992, officially the Treaty of the European Union, the EC member states took the next step in this development. Retaining the existing economic policy jurisdiction of the European Communities as the first pillar of the newly created European Union (EU), the treaty added the justice and home affairs cooperation (its third pillar). But it also established the second pillar, the common foreign and security policy (CFSP), as a constitutional component of the European Union. The CFSP included the clear prospect of a common defense policy for the EU, though this was not yet formulated in concrete terms.

The Maastricht treaty did not create an independent military capacity. Conflicts of interest between the integration supporters led by France and Germany and the integration skeptics siding with Great Britain and the Scandinavian countries—along with the reservations of the United States, which feared NATO might slip into obscurity—left no chance of that. Thus, the EU still had to rely on the WEU as its military arm, though cooperation agreements enabled it to call on the WEU to step in and implement defense policy resolutions.

The lessons of the Balkan War, in which the EU was left standing largely helpless and unable to act, led the states to establish closer ties between the European Union and the WEU in the 1997 Treaty of Amsterdam. Although a consensus could not be reached on the full integration of the WEU into the EU, the WEU's Petersberg tasks—humanitarian and rescue missions, peacekeeping missions, but also crisis management involving combat forces along with peacekeeping measures—have been explicitly adopted into the spectrum of CFSP tasks.

The renewed failure of EU foreign policy in the Kosovo War in 1998, which could only be brought to an end with American intervention at the European Union's request in 1999, highlighted the need for greater efforts by the European Union in the area of security and defense policy. Thanks to an about-face in British politics, which to that point had remained skeptical or rejected outright the thought of an independent European defense system, the British-French summit in Saint-Malo in December 1998 finally managed to launch an independent European defense policy. But to avoid colliding with the structures and interests of NATO, this autonomous defense policy would be limited to those cases in which NATO plays no active role.[72]

---

72 On the shortcomings and future development prospects for the European Security and Defense Policy: Solana 2000, 1–6; Heisbourg 2000; Howorth 2000.

At the summit in Helsinki in December 1999, the EU heads of state and government resolved to establish independent military forces for rapid crisis reaction by 2003. The resolution planned for creating a force of 60,000 ground troops, 30,000 troops in the air force and navy, as well as 100 ships and 400 aircraft.

The WEU was integrated into the EU in July 2001 in the runup to the Treaty of Nice, which then amended the relevant articles of the EU Treaty. To replace the WEU's policy committee, the Nice treaty established a political and security policy committee that meets weekly in Brussels and is prepared to take over crisis management immediately in crisis situations. In a parallel action, new military committees were set up, including the Military Committee, composed of the chiefs of staff or their military representatives, and the Military Staff, comprising up to 135 officers of the EU member states.

The European Council of Laeken determined in December 2002 that the goal of Helsinki had been met early with regard to the preparation of troops. Whether this political determination could be supported with actual substance would be seen soon enough: The European Union police mission in Bosnia and Herzegovina began in January 2003 with a police force of 500 officers from the 15 EU member states and 18 other participating nations.

From the end of March through mid-December 2003, the EU took over a peacekeeping mission for the first time in its history. On the basis of a resolution by the U.N. Security Council, the European Union took command of the Concordia Mission of international troops in the interior of the former Yugoslavian republic of Macedonia. The EU thus relieved NATO but could draw on NATO's means and capabilities in executing the operation. Every EU member state except Denmark and Ireland participated, along with 14 other nations (including the eight new EU members in Eastern Europe).

The first EU military operation without NATO support was Operation Artemis, which took place in the Democratic Republic of Congo from June to September 2003. Initial teething troubles had to be resolved among the military coalitions as well as among the various institutions involved with the European security and defense policy.[73]

73 Seidelmann 2002, 111–124.

But the most significant turning point for the ESDP came when the EU assumed command of the Bosnian peacekeeping force previously led by NATO. In December 2004, the EU took over military peacekeeping operations in the fragile region of Bosnia-Herzegovina. From SFOR came EUFOR, and Mission Althea is by far the largest undertaken by the EU to date.[74]

Thus, the Union seems to have cleared another hurdle on the path to a true common foreign, security and defense policy faster than many—above all the United States—ever expected. The ability for independent military action strengthens both the European Union and the transatlantic alliance. Now it all comes down to the practical feasibility—and the strategic substance—of this new capacity for intervention.

The civilian, or nonmilitary, capacities for crisis management were also strengthened. The EU established a special committee for this purpose to prepare and coordinate missions for police forces, judges and justice officials in crisis regions. At the June 2000 summit at Santa Maria da Feira[75] in Portugal, the EU also committed itself to further action in the realm of civilian crisis management. Member states pledged to provide up to 5,000 police officers for international missions across the range of conflict prevention and crisis management operations by 2003. This goal has since been reached as well.

A long-time point of contention was the question of whether and to what extent the EU can draw on NATO's strategic planning capacities. NATO's means and capabilities are indispensable for the European Union's military interventions in crisis regions. Differences in national interests have prevented a consensus. This led the United States to fear that the EU could build its own planning capacities and thereby separate itself from NATO. By contrast, France—which did not participate in NATO's military integration—saw an opportunity to gain more independence from the United States.

But Turkey opposed the closer union most emphatically because it saw its veto power as a means of pressuring its way into accession negotiations with the EU and furthering the accession process of Cyprus. A December 2002 breakthrough in Laeken came about only

74 Martens 2004, 5.
75 Presidency Conclusions, Santa Maria da Feira European Council, June 19/2000, at http://ue.eu.int/ueDocs/cms_Data/docs/pressData/en/ec/00200-r1.en0.htm (accessed February 4, 2006).

after the Cypriot reunification process was revived under pressure from the EU, and Cyprus was guaranteed entrance into the EU in 2004 (although only the Greek part of Cyprus in actuality, since its population voted in April 2004 against reunification with the Turkish side of the island nation), and America increased its pressure on Turkey. Since that time the EU may rely on the planning capacities of NATO, as was so necessary for the mission in Macedonia.

Approaches for an EU common foreign and security strategy

However, intergovernmentalism and the principle of unanimity in the Council of the EU continue to pose a significant problem for the ESDP as well as the CFSP. To this day, any individual member state can block EU resolutions on both the CFSP and the ESDP. The Constitutional Treaty presented in June 2004 proposes no substantial changes, and national interests diverge widely on the issue of further integration of security policy. Nevertheless, the changes proposed in the Constitutional Treaty do at least reflect the desire of EU member states to move ahead in the area of security policy.

For example, the treaty created the post of EU Minister of Foreign Affairs (Art. III-292 § 3 of the Treaty establishing a Constitution for Europe), combining the previous offices of EU Commissioner for Foreign Affairs and the High Representative for the CFSP. The minister is in charge of the CFSP; the minister's efforts will give the EU a clear foreign policy profile.[76]

And the closer cooperation is giving rise to high hopes within the framework of the CFSP, because it is expected to help overcome differences of interest between the individual member states. The EU Minister of Foreign Affairs will also play a substantial role in initiating and implementing that closer cooperation, which must be open to all EU member states and in which at least one-third of all member

---

76 On the complex topic of the CFSP and ESDP and the changes brought by the EU Constitutional Treaty, see the contributions of Janis A. Emmanouilidis (Die institutionellen Reformen in der Verfassung—die neue Machtarchitektur der Europäischen Union; Der Weg zu einer neuen Integrationslogik—Elemente flexibler Integration in der Europäischen Verfassung) and Franco Algieri/Thomas Bauer (Eine Frage der Macht. Die EU auf dem Weg zum sicherheits- und verteidigungspolitischen Akteur mit globaler Reichweite) in Weidenfeld 2005a.

states must participate. The Constitutional Treaty thus brought some changes—though not a decisive breakthrough, because the European Council still has control over the use of qualified majority votes on matters pertaining to the common foreign and security policy.

The chronic revision of institutional and procedural structures continues to hamper the European Union's ability to act on foreign and security policy, and Europe cannot conduct its foreign affairs effectively. The foreign policy rift in the European Union on the subject of the Iraq war, which culminated in the letter signed by eight heads of state and government in support of U.S. policy and the snubbing of France and Germany, who opposed the war, set back the EU's common foreign and security policy tremendously. To be able to meet the growing foreign policy challenges and act effectively, the European Union must substantially strengthen its CFSP. The goal must be to bridge the chasm between the economic and political dimensions of foreign relations.[77]

This makes it all the more essential for the EU to set forth a clear concept for its security policy strategy. The fundamental principles governing its security policy action and its reactions to international crises must be firmly fixed to enable a broader and more far-reaching consensus among member states. The need became even greater after 10 new members with even more diverse national security interests joined the EU on May 1, 2004.

The April 2003 resolution of the Council of Ministers to authorize Javier Solana, the high representative for the CFSP, to draft a security strategy for the EU was the first step in the right direction. At the European Council summit held June 19–20, 2003, in Thessaloniki, Solana presented the European heads of state and government with his draft. The revised draft was accepted in December 2003 by the heads of state and government at their summit meeting in Brussels.

The security strategy provides a threat analysis for international terrorism, the dispersal of weapons of mass destruction, failed states and organized crime. Furthermore, it identifies poverty in broad sections of the world, Europe's energy dependence and climate change as acute or future threats. The document calls for rapid—and in some cases preventive—action across the foreign policy spectrum to

77 Algieri 1998, 89–120; 2001, 161–202.

fend off threats. This will require further expansion of Europe's military strength.[78]

The United States viewed the European security strategy as an important sign of Europe's willingness to act. With regard to EU foreign policy, the real progress of the European security strategy lies in the fact that the EU–25 were able to agree on a common strategic orientation and framework. Furthermore, the strategy relies on a comprehensive security concept that designates fighting poverty and problems plaguing minorities as security factors right along with nonproliferation regimes and concepts for solving conflicts militarily.

The EU has thus embarked on a new course. In the medium term, the successful development of independent military capacities that do not compete with NATO will give the Europeans substantially greater weight not only in their dealings with the United States in the Atlantic alliance, but also in the global arena. The EU is establishing itself as the only organization worldwide that has a full spectrum of civilian and military options for crisis management at its disposal.

Taking on greater responsibility in global security issues and implementing a more assertive foreign and security policy have become a political imperative for the European Union. Europe's new role in the world of tomorrow includes not only establishing the ability to act effectively on foreign policy, but also creating a European defense identity and the corresponding capabilities.[79]

The goals of the EU and NATO exist in the context of an altered security awareness that includes concepts reaching beyond the military dimension. The division of labor between the enlarged EU and the expanded NATO will shape the European order of the 21st century. It must therefore remain in the interest of the European Union to maintain the transatlantic partnership.

By beginning to develop a European security and defense identity, the EU has already made a step toward taking on greater responsibility and hence toward easing the burden on the United States as well. By deepening its security and defense policy, the EU surmounts its limitations as a civil power and gives itself a new identity.[80] But if the European Union wants credibility in its new foreign policy role, it

78 Solana 2003.
79 Bertelsmann Foundation 2000.
80 On the political science concept of a civil power, see Tewes 1997, 347–359; Maull 1992, 771–786.

must not only restore the confidence in its foreign policy that was damaged in the wake of the Iraq war, but also produce a lasting consensus for a stable internal configuration.

Though the developments of recent years in the area of foreign and security policy are positive overall, they do not suffice to put the European Union on equal footing with the United States in the transatlantic partnership. To achieve that stature, the Europeans must take a common stance when it comes to internal policy challenges; they must successfully move ahead with the integration process, even if that means saying a painful goodbye to individual national interests; and they must find a way, despite their diversity, to develop a European identity as a constitutional community of values.

European challenges— from power game to a constitutional vision

Europe must not only emancipate itself in foreign policy, but also find new answers to challenges at home. The current political problems demand that European politicians come up with strategic responses in four chief areas:
- reforming European institutions;
- further developing the EU toward a coherent political, economic and monetary union;
- stabilizing and integrating Central and Eastern Europe; and
- preserving peace and security on the Continent.

The treaties of Maastricht, Amsterdam and Nice

Completing the Monetary Union and
elevating the status of the European Parliament

The Maastricht Treaty was Europe's first attempt at a comprehensive response to the challenges that ensued when the East-West conflict ended. The negotiations in Maastricht concluded what was at the time the most far-reaching reform of the 1957 Treaties of Rome that established the European Community. When the Maastricht Treaty on European Union was signed, the model of a unified Europe became reality. The European Community—an institution integrated primarily for economic purposes, while relying on political cooperation—was transformed to a Union that also comprised a common foreign and security policy (CFSP) and cooperation in the fields of justice and home affairs (JHA).

The construction of these three pillars of the European Union reflected different views about the finality of the Union. While the European Community (the Union's economic pillar) was organized at the community level, the CFSP and JHA remained a matter of intergovernmental cooperation among member states, though within the formal structure of the Union. As a result, these areas are not subject to the decision-making processes of the EC; in particular, majority decisions are ruled out.

The Maastricht Treaty brought two significant changes to the European Community: First, it established a road map for completion of the Monetary Union in three stages, ending with the introduction of a single currency on January 1, 1999. (The euro had begun circulating as currency among banks as early as 1999; the memorable date of January 1, 2002, merely put its banknotes and coins into general circulation.) Second, it gave the European Parliament a stronger role in the decision-making process, thus substantially elevating its status.

In the arena of the common foreign and security policy, the treaty laid out a plan—though not a schedule—under which the CFSP would first develop a common security policy and then, from that, build a common defense policy that might in time lead to a shared defense force. In the framework of cooperation in justice and home affairs, the member states decided to work more closely together in the areas of asylum, immigration and visa policy; police cooperation and judicial cooperation in civil and criminal matters; and combating terrorism, the illegal drug trade and organized crime. The development of the European police authority Europol also came under JHA.

In sum, the Maastricht Treaty that came into force in 1993 pointed the way toward a qualified consolidation of the European Union. In opposition to the instability that prevailed in Europe after the collapse of the Communist bloc, Maastricht established the goal of a forced—and for monetary policy, irreversible—integration of EU member states.

The next treaty revision, already provided for in Maastricht, took place in June 1997 in Amsterdam. But even before the intergovernmental conference opened, political controversy over employment policy and the stability pact for the monetary union made it clear that any decisions would be confined to the lowest common denominator of agreement. The reforms so urgently needed to gird the EU for expansion into Central and Eastern Europe were shoved into the background. Nevertheless, the Amsterdam Treaty did contain some important points that contributed to consolidating the Union:

- The CFSP was bolstered by the introduction of a high representative for EU foreign policy, who works alongside but independently of the EU Council president. The first to hold this new office was former NATO secretary general Javier Solana of Spain, since then dubbed "Mr. CFSP."
- Cooperation in the fields of justice and home affairs was expanded to include judicial cooperation in civil cases; cooperation in criminal matters was improved and the foundation was laid for joint policies on asylum and immigration.
- Majority decision-making in the European Council was extended, and the European Parliament was granted more codecision rights.
- Of major significance in the medium term was the insertion of flexibility clauses into the treaty. These permit individual groups of member states to move forward with integration in certain policy areas without necessarily including all member states.

Despite partial advances in some policy areas, the Treaty of Amsterdam earns low marks overall. The treaty revisions focused narrowly on areas that required immediate political action. This reliance on advancing by small steps made any consideration of long-term interests only marginally possible. In view of the challenges posed by the Union's imminent enlargement, the treaty's shortcomings outweighed its achievements. The controversial issues were summarily postponed; it would be the task of a future intergovernmental conference to reform EU institutions and prepare the Union for enlargement.[81]

---

81 On the development of the EU between Maastricht and Amsterdam: Weidenfeld 2004a, 15–48; 2005b, 10–50.

In the year 2000, therefore, a new intergovernmental conference met, essentially to deal with the three issues left on the table in Amsterdam: the weighting of votes in the European Council, the extension of majority voting in Council decisions, and the composition and organization of the European Commission. The conference was convened with full awareness that the ability of European institutions to take action had to be ensured even under the conditions of expansion. The task was not merely to remedy existing imbalances but to make the European Union actually capable of functioning even as it expanded.[82]

At the June 2000 European Council held in Santa Maria da Feira, Portugal, the heads of state and government then decided to put on the IGC agenda not just the leftovers of Amsterdam, but also the question of increased cooperation. The IGC thus tackled an agenda that was both clearly delineated and exceptionally fraught with potential conflict.

The main challenge of any such efforts at reform is to strengthen the efficiency and democracy of EU institutions while taking into account and preserving the balance of interests among its member states. At its core, reform has to do with the central architecture of power in Europe, not the trappings of day-to-day politics.

The unfinished federal state as an intermediate stage

In December 2000, after hard-fought negotiations, the representatives of the EU member states reached an agreement. The Treaty of Nice that entered into force on February 1, 2003, represented the fourth major revision of the European treaties within 15 years. However, neither the composition of the Commission nor the weighting of votes in the Council of Ministers were resolved in a way that would significantly enhance the workings of a European Union comprising as many as 28 member states.[83]

In the Council, a triple majority—of votes, states and citizens—is now required for a qualified majority decision. If anything, the Treaty of Nice made EU decision-making processes even less transparent;

---

82 Bertelsmann Europa-Kommission 2000; Weidenfeld 1994, 1998.
83 For a detailed discussion of the institutional changes: Giering 2001, 51–144.

structures within the European Union proliferate as the degree of integration escalates. This once again raises the question of legitimation.

At the same time, the European Council did not have the courage to clearly extend the principle of majority rule. Important areas such as CFSP, tax policy, social and structural policy remain bound by unanimity—a European anachronism that the heads of state and government quite openly celebrated as a triumph of national interests at work.

The workings of the European Commission likewise escaped reforms that would enhance its future ability to act. The principle that each member state appoints at least one commissioner was retained, at least for the time being. No decisive breakthrough was achieved that would lead to a commission whose size does not depend on the number of member states.

The heads of state and government dutifully applauded the Nice summit as a success. But the challenges of EU enlargement and the conclusive establishment of the euro as the common currency should have compelled them to make the sort of trailblazing decisions that cannot be guided by individual wants. Instead, national interests elbowed the EU aside in a way reminiscent of the old patterns of intergovernmental politics in the 1960s.[84]

In Nice, the "unfinished federal state"[85] of Europe turned into a bazaar of national interests. Despite all the pre-Nice visions, the Council of Europe once again displayed a hallmark of European politics: Whenever matters of substance are at stake, national habits and long traditions make themselves felt. In particular, the matter of prestige disrupted the leadership duo of France and Germany. As soon as they fell out of stride, every conceivable conflict erupted: the small against the large, the small and the large among themselves, the "old" against the "new" member states. Despite 50 years of striving for integration, the Machiavellian craft of interest-driven power games is still at work in Europe. This could even intensify with the recent enlargements and those yet to come.

---

84 Cf. the empty chair policy and the resulting Luxembourg compromise of 1966; among others, see Giering 1997, 62ff.
85 Hallstein 1994.

Possibly the most important decision at Nice was to initiate a post-Nice process, to continue until 2004, that would establish a division of tasks between the European Union and its member states in accord with the subsidiarity principle; determine the conclusive treaty status of the Charter of Fundamental Rights, which had merely been declared in Nice; simplify the complicated and confusing Community treaties; and determine the future role of the national parliaments in the European architecture. Thus, Nice in its turn rang in another round of reforms.

The negotiations in Nice highlighted the core of the debate on consolidating the Union: Not all EU member states can meet the objectives of integration at the same time, and not all want to meet them. A much more serious problem also came to light: Many of its citizens find the European Union quite incomprehensible. To their eyes, the complicated mechanisms of Europe's decision-making and administrative structures primarily serve the interests of European bureaucracy and have little to do with regulating their own everyday lives.

The new Europe is moving too fast for its citizens

The process of European unification started at the top, while enjoying the broad-based support of the citizens of the original member states. But as integration progressed, governments increasingly neglected to consolidate the democratic legitimacy of European institutions in the eyes of their citizens.

As a result, the public debate on ratifying the Treaty of Nice did not really center on the objective discussion of the treaty's contents. Rather, the treaty's incomprehensible bulk made it a magnet for the vague worries, fears and reservations of the citizens of Europe.

The half-hearted efforts to win public acceptance are particularly striking because they tally with the attitude of growing disillusionment with politics apparent throughout Western Europe. Barraged by revelations of corruption and abuse of power, many citizens have come to believe that political and economic decision-makers merely serve the complicated system they themselves created and have lost sight of the actual interests of their constituents.

As a result, the EU must now tackle, at a different level, the same phenomenon that underlies the shift in domestic policy in the United

States. Many Americans believe that the traditional practices of political decision-making have become an impenetrable labyrinth, and they have deep-seated doubts about its legitimacy and efficiency. For the average American, Washington has become a synonym for over-organized and useless bureaucracy—an image that Brussels has held among critics of European integration for quite some time.

Ordinary citizens on both sides of the Atlantic have grown increasingly intolerant of unfathomable strategies presented as the solutions to national and international problems. Hence, it is imperative that both the United States and the European Union make fundamental changes to their political and administrative structures, with acceptance and efficiency as their benchmarks. If they do not succeed, the transatlantic partners face a growing risk that they will lose their capacity for action both at home and in the international arena.

The EU constitutional convention

General revision of the EU for greater transparency, democracy and efficiency

The December 2000 treaty revisions in Nice aimed to reshape the institutions and decision-making procedures of the EU to carry it into the future. The political reality after Nice, however, was a long way from the intended blend of efficiency, enlargement and close connection between the EU and its citizens.

For this reason, the European Council resumed the post-Nice process in December 2001. Laying out a broad agenda in the Laeken Declaration, it committed the European Union to a general revision in the direction of greater democracy, efficiency and transparency. It even cautiously considered the possibility of a European constitution—a concept that had been practically taboo in European politics until then. To prepare for this major undertaking, it assigned a European convention the task of drawing up proposals for the reform of the European Union.

For the first time in the history of European integration, a convention assembled to lay the groundwork for treaty revisions. The outcome would be presented to an intergovernmental conference that would then negotiate and implement the convention's recommendations.[86]

The convention that began its work on February 28, 2002, was comprised of 105 members, including representatives of the member states' governments, the national parliaments, the European parliament, the Commission, and the governments and parliaments of the 13 candidate countries. Former French president Valéry Giscard d'Estaing chaired the convention, which took up the following central issues:

- the apportionment and delimitation of competences between the Union and the member states;
- the interrelationship among the Union's institutions, with a view to achieving greater democracy, transparency and efficiency;
- the Union's political instruments and decision-making processes; and
- the simplification of the existing treaties and incorporation of their most important components in a single fundamental treaty.

The last of these, a general revision of the existing treaties, became the centerpiece of the convention's agenda. By the time it adjourned on July 10, 2003, the convention had held 27 plenary sittings and 50 presidium meetings.[87] It completed its major task—preparation for the next intergovernmental conference—on July 18, 2003, when it submitted the Draft Treaty establishing a Constitution for Europe[88] to the Italian Council Presidency. It had accomplished what at first looked nearly impossible: bringing together the existing treaties into a single constitutional document. Among the key achievements of this document is that it elevates the EU Charter of Fundamental Rights to the status of a binding legal document. Other prominent outcomes were its extension of majority decision-making in the Coun-

---

86 For a comprehensive analysis of the Convention itself and a compilation of all its official documents, see Giering 2003; see also Reform Spotlights of the Center for Applied Policy Research, Munich, at www.cap-lmu.de/publikationen/spotlights.php (accessed February 1, 2005).

87 Meyer/Hölscheidt 2003, 336–346; also Göler/Jopp 2003, 35–46. On the chronology of the Convention, cf. Metz/Notz 2003.

88 See also the report from the chair of the convention to the president of the European Council, Brussels, July 18, 2003, EU Document CONV 851/03. The draft of the Constitutional Treaty itself is available online: http://european-convention.eu.int/docs/Treaty/cv00850.en03.pdf (accessed February 2, 2006).

cil of Ministers and its enhancement of parliament's role in the EU legislative process. In many respects, the document fell short; problems accumulated over 50 years of European integration proved resistant to reform. But on the whole, the convention had taken a great step forward. Its achievements went far beyond anything an intergovernmental conference could have accomplished on its own.[89]

The Treaty establishing a Constitution for Europe

A European compromise

The Intergovernmental Conference began on October 4, 2003, with the task of finalizing and approving the draft treaty revisions. But it also had to tackle a number of open questions. During the EC summit meetings in Brussels in December 2003, the European heads of state and government could not resolve the important issue of majority decision-making within the Council. The convention had proposed a simple, plausible system—qualified majority voting, also known as the double majority—under which more than half of EU member states must approve a proposed law and these states must represent more than 60 percent of the EU population. The Nice criterion, which weighted the votes of member states according to their population, was eliminated. But in the negotiations, Poland and Spain insisted on retaining the Nice formula, which gave each of them 27 votes—only two less than the "big four" (Germany, France, Great Britain and Italy)—even though their populations were significantly smaller.

Several months later, the member states agreed on a compromise: raising the threshold for the double majority. The Constitution was adopted by the heads of state and government on June 17/18, 2004, and signed with much fanfare on October 29, 2004, in Rome. This set the clock ticking for the national ratification processes. Ultimately, however, the critical question will be what the citizens of Europe think. Only if they give their approval and support can the Constitution establish the identity of a unified Europe. The road is rocky; the politicians clearly have not figured out how to make the draft Consti-

89 Weidenfeld 2003a, 13–24.

tution accessible to the public. They paid the price when the citizens of France and The Netherlands—EU founding states at that—clearly rejected the EU Constitution. Almost 55 percent of French voters said "Non" to the treaty document in a referendum on May 28, 2005, and three days later a solid 62 percent of the Dutch chimed in with "Nee." The fact that the German Bundestag had overwhelmingly ratified the EU Constitution on May 27, with 569 votes in favor, 23 opposed and two abstentions, did little to soften the blow. Thunderstruck, the French president initiated a cabinet shakeup and the governments of Great Britain, Denmark and Sweden indefinitely postponed their ratification plans.

It will take an intensive, long-term public relations campaign to carry the Constitutional Treaty into the hearts and minds of citizens at the European, national, regional and local levels. Only if the campaign succeeds will the European Constitution accomplish its intended purpose of advancing European integration.

The initial outlook is sobering: The Treaty establishing a Constitution for Europe does not incorporate all the needed reforms. Its sheer scope—448 articles—threatens to overwhelm EU citizens. Convoluted in structure and difficult to read, the document does little to help citizens understand the European Union and its systems. Foreign and security policy-making still largely relies on the unanimity principle; the European Council retains the right to nominate the Commission president; reforms to the Council of Ministers stop short of what is needed. All of these aspects run counter to the efficiency, capacity to act and connection to citizens that the enlarged European Union requires.

The Constitutional Treaty nonetheless achieved much that seemed impossible not long ago. The convention paved the way. Most notably, its participants combined the previous treaties in a single document that also incorporates the Charter of Fundamental Rights. Other highlights include defining the codecision rights of the EU parliament and instituting majority rule in the Council of Ministers as part of established legislative procedures. The document remedies important defects in the Treaty of Nice.

To a large extent, the convention succeeded because—unlike the treaties of Maastricht, Amsterdam and Nice, which were drawn up in intergovernmental conferences—the Constitutional Treaty was developed by a body that included government representatives, European

Parliament members, Commission representatives and delegates from the national parliaments. This structure, which had already proved its worth in the convention that wrote the Charter of Fundamental Rights, did a great deal to enhance the transparency and democratic legitimation of the outcome.

In a detailed analysis, the Constitutional Treaty must be evaluated against a number of criteria: It must strengthen the European identity of EU citizens, refine the assignment of competences within the EU, guarantee efficient political management and capacity for action, and ultimately enable the text itself to sustain dynamic further development.[90]

One objective of the convention was to enhance the political identification of citizens with the EU through the following features of the draft treaty:

- merger of the existing treaties into a single document;
- conferral on the Union of a single legal personality;
- incorporation of the Charter of Fundamental Rights into the constitutional text; and
- introduction of a solidarity clause for mutual assistance in case of terrorist attacks and natural disasters.

Crucial aspects of the draft Constitution

On the whole, however, the authors did not manage to write a clear and concise document. To grasp the goals and limits, rights and responsibilities of the European Union, its citizens must read all 448 articles of the Constitution. The host of protocols and annexes attached to the document only adds to the bewildering thicket of constitutional provisions.

With regard to the division of tasks and delimitation of competences that govern relations between the Union and its member states, it should be counted as progress that the first part of the draft document specifies the policy areas where the Union has the sole right to act, where competences are shared between the Union and the member states, and where the EU can only take supporting or coordinating actions. Special provisions address the coordination of economic

90 Cf. Weidenfeld 2005a.

and employment policy; the common foreign, security and defense policy; and the region of freedom, security and justice the EU is striving to create.

Despite this apparent delimitation of competences in Part I of the Constitution, problems arise because the delimitation is not really unambiguous. Rather, additional provisions follow in Part III that specify who can act with what means in which policy areas. Because these provisions do not correspond to the system outlined in Part I, the document cannot be said to establish a clear structure.

One of the most important aspects of the draft Constitution is its institutional restructuring of the Union. Its future institutional power structures must do justice in equal measure to the legitimation strands of the Union as an association of states and an association of citizens. But when it comes to defining and executing strategic tasks, the same structures must also guarantee the capacity for action of a Union enlarged to 25 states and more. The draft Constitution made some progress here. Above all, the introduction of a European Council president elected by the heads of state and government is a positive step toward continuity, visibility and coherence in EU representation. Another is the proposed post of European minister of foreign affairs, with greater power than today's "Mr. CFSP," High Representative Javier Solana.

The European Commission also gets a makeover. In view of the EU's enlargement by 10 states and more to come, the current provision that each member state supplies at least one commissioner was in urgent need of reform. Under the Constitution, starting in 2014 the number of members (including the Commission president and the foreign minister) will correspond to two-thirds of the number of member states. This will ensure the Commission's long-term ability to act even when the Union expands to more than 25 members. Linked to the trimmer Commission is a stronger role for its president, who can organize the Commission and allocate portfolios based on objective considerations instead of national proportionality and may also ask individual Commission members to resign because of bad behavior.

Despite these positive changes, weaknesses and shortcomings remain. The unclear definition of competences threatens to make the president of the European Council a puppet of that body as well as a competitor to the future EU foreign minister in the area of foreign affairs. The foreign minister, in turn, has an ambiguous role in the Commission, which can put either the Commission or the European Council at a disadvantage. Above all, however, the institutional balance of power is called into question because the European Council appoints both its own president and the Commission president. It would be preferable for the Commission president to be elected by the European Parliament and then confirmed by the European Council. That is the only way to strengthen the legitimacy and power base of the Commission and its president, advance the personalization of European politics and consolidate the importance of European elections as an act of choice and control for its citizens.

In the matter of legislative procedures, the Constitutional Treaty contains a number of significant improvements. For example, the qualified majority vote is established as a decision-making procedure in the Council of Ministers, and the European parliament has been given a general right of codecision. Exceptions to which the unanimity principle still applies in the Council will have to be explicitly listed. In the end, this will substantially improve an enlarged Union's ability to act. Regrettably, however, the qualified majority vote was not introduced as a Council decision-making procedure in the areas of joint foreign and security policy and in trade and tax policy. Especially in foreign and security affairs, this retention of the unanimity principle will lead to blockades in a Union with 25 and more member states. Ultimately these blockades can only be resolved by resorting to differentiated integration—possibly even outside the domain of the new Constitution.

Another important innovation that likewise falls under the heading of differentiated integration is the long-overdue recognition of the Euro Group as an independent body with representatives only from the countries that have adopted the euro as their single currency. This group will now be represented internally and externally by a "Mr./Ms. Euro" elected every two and one-half years.

However, a European constitution cannot be a static document. In form and content, it must be able to adapt to the process of further integration. To that end, the Constitution expands and specifies the contractual nature of a differentiated integration process that emerges particularly in the field of security and defense policy. For the future, this affords possibilities for the ongoing and increasingly structured cooperation of individual groups of member states.

As a treaty, too, the Constitution remains dynamic. Constitutional amendments are explicitly included in the plan, although they in turn must also clear the formal hurdle of ratification in all the member states. But in contrast to the current treaties, the Constitution will also provide a procedure by which a member state that persistently rejects an amendment can withdraw from the Union. Of course, individual states could also use the availability of this option as a means of exerting political pressure.

Overcoming the constitutional crisis

But what alternatives remain for the EU if the European Constitution cannot enter into force? Political decision-makers and EU experts agree in principle that the Treaty of Nice is not the suitable framework for preparing a European Union of 25 (and soon more) member states to meet future challenges.

A pragmatic option would be to secure the central features of the constitutional innovations with regard to efficiency, democracy and transparency and incorporate them into the existing treaties. To do this, it would be necessary to identify the central reforms of the Constitution and to bring them together in the shape of a treaty amending the Treaty of Nice. Such changes would affect both the Treaty on the European Union (EU Treaty) and the Treaty establishing the European Community (EC Treaty). In the tradition of the Single European Act and the treaty revisions of Maastricht, Amsterdam and Nice, such a treaty would have to be adopted by an intergovernmental conference and ratified in the member states according to their national provisions.

The reform of the current treaties on the basis of the innovations contained in the Constitutional Treaty would affect the following core areas:

- reform of the EU's institutional system;
- further development of its decision-making and voting procedures;
- reform and enhancement of the instruments of differentiated integration; and
- a series of structural provisions.

Reform of the institutional system

The central institutional reforms of the Constitutional Treaty should be incorporated into the current treaties. Chief among these are appointing an elected president of the European Council, creating the position of a Union Minister for Foreign Affairs and an administrative structure to support it (European External Action Service), introducing a team presidency in the Council of Ministers, establishing a long-term presidency in the Euro Group, reducing the size of the Commission and strengthening its presidency.

This personalization of the European leadership architecture makes it possible to assign responsibilities more clearly on the EU level and enhances the continuity, visibility and coherence of European policy-making.

Further development of decision-making and voting procedures

If the EU is to remain capable of taking action and enhance its democratic legitimation, it must reform the decision-making and voting procedures in both the Council of Ministers and the European Parliament and assign a prominent role to the national parliaments.

The introduction of the double majority voting procedure constitutes a milestone in the development of the European Union. Applying the number of citizens and the number of states as the basis for decision-making in the Council of Ministers reflects the two strands of EU legitimation. This voting procedure makes it more difficult to form blockade coalitions of member states and easier to form constructive majorities. The extension of majority decisions in the Council of Ministers—from 137 to 181 instances—is crucial to the problem-solving competence of an expanded EU and should also be taken into account in a revision of the Treaty of Nice.

The rights of national parliaments (via the early warning mechanism) should be enhanced, and elements of direct democracy (citizens' initiatives) should be introduced. Furthermore, the budgetary powers and the codecision rights of the European Parliament in the legislative process should be strengthened (extension of codecision).

The interests of the member states in the enlarged European Union are becoming increasingly diverse. For this reason, strategies of differentiated integration are of paramount importance. Even in the past, blockades or the lack of political will in certain member states in the fields of monetary, internal and social policy were overcome with the tools of differentiation, thereby promoting the process of integration.

The amendment of the current treaties should take over the reforms of the existing flexibility instruments set forth in the Constitutional Treaty (enhanced cooperation) and adopt new instruments especially in the area of common security and defense policy (Permanent Structured Cooperation, EU Missions, cooperation within the European Defense Agency).

The open method of coordination should be anchored in the revised Treaty of Nice as it is in the Constitution. This method reduces the role of the EU to setting target dates for the member states and monitoring compliance with the agreements. Therein lies its central advantage: The member states must implement national action plans and are in transparent competition with one another.

Structural provisions

In addition to the institutional changes, the reform of the decision-making and voting procedures, and the development of the instruments of differentiated integration, essential structural provisions of the European Constitution should form part of the amendments to the existing treaties. These include

- legally binding incorporation of the Charter of Fundamental Rights into the Treaty of Nice. A reference to the legally binding nature of the Charter (instead of the complete text) would suffice;
- introduction of competence categories that would define areas where the Union has exclusive authority, responsibilities that are shared by the Union and the member states, and areas where the Union can only act to complement or support actions by the member state;
- incorporation of the "passerelle" or bridging clauses, which will make it possible to improve the decision-making procedures in

the Council of Ministers, the co–decision-making powers of the European Parliament, or certain internal policies without convening an intergovernmental conference;

- reform of the treaty revision procedure, so that future changes to primary law are not decided merely by government representatives behind closed doors, but are publicly debated and concluded in the framework of a convention that also includes representatives of the national parliaments, the European Parliament and the European Commission;
- incorporation of the solidarity clause, which provides for joint action if a member state is the object of a terrorist attack or the victim of a natural or man-made disaster. This clause has already proved its worth in the EU response to the terrorist attacks in Madrid and London; and
- introduction of a mutual assistance obligation under which the EU member states commit themselves to aid and assistance, including military action if necessary, if a member state is the victim of armed aggression on its territory.

These changes to certain provisions of the EU and EC Treaty of Nice could preserve the central innovations of the Constitution even without embarking on a constitutional reformulation of European primary law. The restricted revision of the current treaties by an intergovernmental conference will strengthen both the EU's ability to act and its democratic legitimacy. At the same time, it deliberately eschews a strikingly symbolic emphasis on the treaty-based nature of integration.

Further reform of the European Union

Integration has reached a saturation point that forces every advance to be justified anew. Therefore, even with its Constitution, the European Union is under constant pressure to reform. Integration is proceeding as a process of gradual adjustment to new goals and tasks. Ever since the founding of the European Coal and Steel Community, each step of reform has been characterized by the often-difficult negotiation of compromise among the member states. The outcome of this negotiation logic is a multilevel system in which various planes of action overlap in a complicated pattern. This has given rise to a confusing web of intermingled jurisdictions. Even within the individual areas of responsibility, rules and regulations were often further differentiated and dealt with by different bodies. As a result, it is difficult to understand exactly what the competences of today's European Union actually are.

The stakes are high. Welfare and security—traditional and elementary functions of the state—can no longer be achieved without the European Union. The policies, processes and institutions of integration belong to the substance of European politics; they are not frills. Each major issue confronted by the Continent's societies also raises the question of European governance, for hardly any issue fails to affect Europeans as an interconnected whole.

Thus, the challenges of international terrorism unequivocally demand action at the European level. It would be inconceivable to redefine the connection between internal and external security were it not for the links between CFSP and ESDP, along with the communication and coordination procedures developed since 1999 in the fields of law enforcement and internal affairs. Europe must act in this arena; otherwise, its strengths—its many and varied territories, interconnections and systems of public order—will be exploited as weaknesses.

Furthermore, expectations for tough security in Europe have risen in the aftermath of September 11. The states of Europe must be able to secure the peace and curb civil wars and violence on their own doorstep and under their own leadership—but that is not all. They also need the wherewithal to protect their interests, their values and their partners wherever these are fundamentally in jeopardy. Europe cannot guarantee security without contributions from the EU states. Equally obvious, however, is that over the long haul none of the states can sustain adequate capacities on their own.

The European Council had set itself the goal of establishing a territory of freedom, security and justice by the year 2004. Joint decisions pertaining to asylum, visas and migration, along with the creation of the European police authority Europol and the common prosecuting authority Eurojust have indeed advanced integration to a new plateau. But the journey will not end here. Additional projects consistent with creating a common internal security zone—such as establishing a European border patrol, developing Eurojust into a

European public prosecutor's office with limited rights to conduct investigations in the member states, and expanding the operational rights of Europol—are already on the horizon.

If the transnational consequences of free movement within the single market and of Union citizenship come under the governance of the EU, then full participation of the European Parliament in legislation and parliamentary control of the executive should also be secured. The future status of the Charter of Fundamental Rights plays an important role. The Charter protects citizens against infringements of their rights by Community institutions. It is the job of the EC Court of Justice to guarantee the necessary rule of law. The apportionment of responsibilities between member states and the EU must be done with particular care when it comes to policies on fundamental rights, an area that affects citizens directly.

Thus, Europe still has work to do. The Economic and Monetary Union was brought to completion when the first European currency was issued on January 1, 2002. But the new security tasks had already pushed their way to the forefront of an agenda studded with major tasks and ambitious plans:

- consolidation of the EU after the May 2004 accession of the 10 new member states from eastern and southern Europe;
- continuation of EU structural reforms, as laid out on July 18, 2003, by the Convention on the Future of Europe, chaired by Valéry Giscard d'Estaing, and incorporated in modified form in the European Constitution;
- swift development of the European Union as a security community by establishing an area of freedom, security and justice;
- steady development of the common foreign, security and defense policy; and
- completion of the process launched by the European Council in Lisbon in March 2000 to develop a modern information society that would make the EU the "most competitive and dynamic knowledge-based economy in the world."

If the decision-makers of Europe want to accomplish these tasks, they will need broad approval from the citizenry. To win acceptance of European governance in this key phase of integration policy, they must set clear political priorities and achieve better apportionment of political responsibility.

Onward through dynamism and differentiation

The central topic of capacity for action will become even more crucial as today's Europe, consisting of 25 member states and some 450 million residents, expands to embrace 28 or more states. The decisive question is how a community of states boasting such tremendous diversity—political, economic, cultural—can possibly be organized.

A careful study of the history of European unification reveals that the key to success is differentiation: allowing for different forms of organization, putting measures into action at different paces. The larger and more diverse the territory to be integrated, the greater the necessity for differentiation. In the future, domestic policy and judicial policy, common foreign and security policy, economic and monetary union and the single market will not all involve the same member states. Such a complicated system can only remain organized, however, if it follows a calculated course. Mere happenstance will not do. The European Union therefore needs a plan that can organize integration at a high level but also modulate its advance.

European policy debates should therefore address the question of what a larger Europe where readiness for integration varies widely must look like. For in an enlarged European Union, innovative steps toward integration will be possible—even more often than in the past—only in combination with a greater variation in their pace. This will particularly affect policy areas in which a continued requirement for unanimity stands in the way of common progress. Where the differentiated circles of advancement overlap, integration's center of gravity will then automatically be evident.[91] The EU needs the maneuver room of differentiation so that the variously strong ambitions and potential of the member states can be put to work for the benefit of Europe.

---

91 Cf. speech by German foreign minister Joschka Fischer at Humboldt University in Berlin on May 12, 2000: "From Confederacy to Federation—Thoughts on the finality of European integration." http://www.auswaertiges-amt.de/www/de/infoservice/download/pdf/reden/redene/r000512b-r1008e.pdf (accessed February 1, 2006).

The EU as a community of values and a constitutional community—the search for a European identity

With the Treaty establishing a Constitution for Europe signed by the European heads of state and government in 2004, a piece of shared constitutional identity can emerge.[92] The Single European Act of 1986, the Maastricht Treaty of 1992 and the Amsterdam Treaty of 1997 allowed a new set of facts to take shape that already put the question of Europe's "becoming a state" in a new light. But in this regard, the Constitutional Treaty for Europe is a milestone. The more rights the European Union attains, the more natural it becomes to perceive it as an actor with the stature of a national state. It is hardly likely that Europe will reach this status and achieve full European integration simultaneously. An understanding must first be reached on the path and goals of European integration.

As the European Union prepares for the internal and foreign policy challenges of integration, its decision-makers must reorganize its internal political system and assemble the material prerequisites for taking action in foreign policy. At the same time, the debate about the finality of European integration, now rekindled, must continue with a new dynamic.

For the evaluation of the future course of transatlantic relations, the question arises of how the United States stands with regard to the European Union's integration and enlargement, what advantages it expects to gain, and what conditions Europe must satisfy to be perceived as an equal partner on the other side of the Atlantic.

---

92 For the full text of the Treaty establishing a Constitution for Europe signed at a celebration in Rome on October 29, 2004, see the Web site of the Council of the European Union, http://ue.eu.int/cms3_fo/showPage.asp?lang=en&id=735&mode=g&name= (accessed February 1, 2006). For more on the topic, see also Weidenfeld 2005a.

America and the EU of the future—
European integration from an American perspective

Advantages of an enlarged European Union

At first glance, it appears paradoxical: Of all the times to raise the question of Europe's leadership role, the Americans choose a period of profound change on that continent. Beset by challenges at home and abroad, the global power is increasingly pressing the Europeans to play a greater role in solving the world's problems.

Granted, disagreement on the appropriate way to share military, political and financial burdens runs like a red thread through the history of the Western alliance. But the end of the Cold War and the repercussions of September 11 have given this dispute an entirely new quality. The absolute dominance of the U.S. arsenal has been transformed into mere relative superiority now that nuclear deterrence has faded to the point of insignificance. And since the September 11 attacks, the American public has exerted an unprecedented amount of pressure on its government to channel all available resources into meeting the immense security challenges it faces.

Thus, the United States has a definite stake in the European Union's progress toward speaking with one voice politically and militarily, or at least getting the chorus of voices in tune. The caveats from the U.S. side—that a stronger European Union may become more independent (e.g., in its defense policy) and perhaps end its alliance with the United States—will continue. But as the problems mount and the need to share the burden grows, the unequivocal advocates of European integration will keep the upper hand in American policy-making for the foreseeable future.

This also applies to economic relations, for here too the United States will profit when advances in European integration mean that the slowest ship in the European convoy can no longer block forward-looking strategies of transatlantic economic partnership.

Just as the deepening of the EU is in the vital interests of the United States, so too is its enlargement. The absorption of new members from Eastern Europe will greatly increase their inner stability and significantly reduce the possibility of crises and conflicts in the region.

Some in the United States still fear that the European Union could use the integration of Eastern Europe to turn that area into a

European "chasse gardée," at least economically. But these considerations remain secondary to the strategic advantages of EU membership for the Eastern countries.

The problems of reconstruction and postwar order in Afghanistan and Iraq prove that the United States depends on a close working relationship with the Europeans. Neither the ill feelings resulting from the Iraq war nor Washington's distinction between an "old" and a "new" Europe can alter that fact. For the EU, busy with the internal, often petty quarrels of European integration, the United States, as its chief partner, plays an important role by constantly reminding it not to forget the great international challenges.

Europe as an equal partner of the United States

Simply because of its economic strength, today's Europe—whether it knows it or not—bears worldwide responsibilities. Together with the United States, it already has become the most important focus of global hopes for democracy and economic progress. In the future, America increasingly will expect Europe to take on political responsibilities commensurate with its status as an economic world power.

The Europeans, for their part, will have it drummed into them again and again—even as the EU deepens and widens—that the United States is their chief partner. At first, Europe's familiar equilibrium reflex will play an important role: Whenever a European nation fears a sustained shift in the economic and political balance on the continent that may not work in its favor, it tries to bring the United States into play to maintain equilibrium.

In the current global political arena, however, calling in the United States as referee and guarantor of equilibrium within Europe is an outdated tactic that the United States will no longer accept. In the last 50 years, Western Europe has achieved a level of political and economic stability that makes unilateral efforts by the United States to guarantee peace within Europe and to ensure a balance among the European partners superfluous. The United States no longer wishes to serve as patron saint of the new European order, as it did in the postwar era. It is far more interested in a symmetrical partnership that includes Europe as an equal counterpart in international politics, with all the rights—and especially the new obligations—this entails.

Today, the European Union has ample potential to take on this new role. One requirement for tapping this potential is that the Europeans are politically aware of the new international challenges that have emerged since the end of the Cold War and the September 11 attacks. If they fail to react to these challenges, or if their response falls short, the transatlantic community is at risk of permanent erosion. In its quest for partners who will share the burden, the United States will increasingly cast its nets outside Europe.

None of the developments within the European Community and the European Union in recent decades has had any effect on the fundamental asymmetry in Euro-American relations. Europe has gained economic strength and become an increasingly muscular rival to the United States, but politically America's dominance in determining and implementing Western strategies has remained intact even when the United States opted to delegate responsibility to the Europeans.

The recently accomplished reform of the European Union must do its part to overcome this asymmetry. The transatlantic perspective must be an integral part of further efforts toward European integration, for it alone enables the European partners to recognize the global coordinates of reforms that many in Europe regard as a purely European affair. Including the United States does not, as many mistakenly think, mean allowing the United States to make decisions in Brussels—to sit in on the cabinet discussions of the European government, so to speak. Rather, coordinating further steps toward integration means working out in advance what consequences the objectives of European integration—such as the progressive framing of a common foreign, security and defense policy—will have for Europe's main partner. It also means including in the equation cooperation with the United States as an equal power. Only this will enable the European Union to look beyond Europe's borders when future reforms become necessary and to create a new European order with a modern, international outlook.

From an American perspective, the breadth and complexity of the changes in Europe no doubt cause confusion and raise questions about the transatlantic partner's future identity. Many in the United States attempt to compare the development of the European Union with the birth of their own nation, but predictions based on this are bound to mislead. No matter how close-knit the European Union becomes, for the foreseeable future Europe will remain a community of nation states, while the United States was never a nation state in the traditional sense of the term.

Requirements for an eye-to-eye partnership

The challenge in Europe goes beyond the undertaking chronicled in U.S. history, that of regulating the balance of rights between the individual and the state, with the demands of the latter increasing naturally as society becomes more highly organized. Europe must additionally go through the painful process of transferring centuries-old prerogatives from the individual states into the hands of the Union. This process takes time. Even the hard realities of world politics cannot hasten it—a fact often brought bitterly home to the Americans when they have demanded a common European response to urgent problems that called for a transatlantic solution.

Given this different degree of organization, from the U.S. standpoint any realistic assessment of what the Europeans can do must keep in mind the lingering asymmetry between the United States and Europe. The Western community—the North Atlantic alliance—still consists of one major world power and an array of small and medium-sized states across the ocean.

From the outset, the United States has given its sustained support to the (Western) European states' efforts toward integration. It took in stride the growth of a potential competitor because it expected Europe to take some of the weight of global problems from its shoulders. But this hope has not yet been fulfilled. European integration has turned out to be an economic success story, but politically Europe has not even come close to matching the United States strength for strength. It has hobbled along behind, chiefly because political union so far has not kept pace with economic integration.

In tackling the question of an appropriate form of organization for the Western partnership, then, the Europeans must first take stock of their political union. The more effectively the European Union can organize itself, the easier it will be for the United States to make a long-term commitment to Europe. The EU must draw on its economic might to fortify its foreign and security policy so as to strengthen the European pillar of the alliance.

Up to now, the United States has not been able to enter into the dialogue between equal partners so essential to a durable and vital alliance. When it asks what action the West should take, Washington still hears a chorus of different European responses. It remains to be seen whether the new EU foreign minister is up to the task of generating a degree of clarity for this important partner—and soon. The United States itself can do little to accelerate the clarification process in Europe. It has learned in the past that Europe's internal discourse is not susceptible to outside influence. Attempts to push through American objectives by means of close bilateral cooperation with individual EU member states have proved just as ineffective as occasional pressure on the European Commission. Until the Europeans rise to a new level, the partners will remain at odds.

5 Re-establishing the transatlantic community

By the time of the Iraq war, if not before, it became clear that transatlantic relationships were changing. It remains to be seen whether the United States and Europe will draw closer again or continue to drift apart. This chapter outlines options for reorganizing the transatlantic structures in security and defense policy. Next, it illuminates the interests of the United States and Europe as partners and rivals in world trade. Finally, it focuses on examples of successful cooperation in the cultural arena and on transnational problem areas such as migration and environmental protection.

The reorganization of transatlantic structures in security and defense policy

The most recent transatlantic crisis, which began in the runup to the third Gulf war, will reverberate for some time. The crisis intensified when the United States invaded Iraq. At least from the German perspective, it was not officially defused until Chancellor Gerhard Schröder visited President Bush in September 2003. It was a crisis of extraordinarily grave proportions.[93]

As Europe and America embark on a new era of transatlantic cooperation, the political elite in Europe and America must summon a degree of leadership and vision equal to that displayed by the founders of the postwar order. Transatlantic relationships will inevitably find a new direction. But whether the precious stuff of transatlantic friendship survives, develops and functions under new conditions will depend on how the different components of the relationship evolve.

93 On this topic, see also Szabo 2004.

The war with Iraq is one of the most visible symbols of this turning point in history. It brought massive changes to America's relations with the rest of the world and to relations within Europe. Future historians will characterize the time period between the attack on the World Trade Center and the Iraqi war as the beginning of a new era. They will see the end of the East-West conflict as the incubation period for a turning point whose full consequences were not reducible to one concept by its contemporaries. Unsurprisingly, the political response worldwide has been erratic and confused, reflected in intellectual commentary. The war exposed a lack of orientation. Where it was once fashionable to speak of a paradigm shift, one now soberly acknowledges paradigm atrophy.

The demands of our era are too high; too much must be resolved in too many places, and too many previously legitimate assumptions appear to have become irrelevant. Almost everything that seemed to lend world politics the image of a reasonably reliable order is no longer valid.

Consequences of the September 11 attacks and the Iraqi war

The attacks on September 11, 2001, and the Iraqi war present seven consequences for the future of international politics:

1. In the beginning there was terrorism. This is not to say that everything is a consequence of terrorism, but the attacks of September 11 released forces, triggered traumas, and made us all look into the abyss of serious dangers that were previously hidden and more or less ignored. The end of the Cold War and the dissipation of communist ideology and its goal of world domination left smoldering conflicts in the background. Religious fundamentalism, volatile ethnic tensions and heated nationalism had long been contained within the iron grip of bipolarity. Now they were suddenly set free. A new aggressiveness caught the world community by surprise, from the Balkans to the Caucasus, Afghanistan to Pakistan, Iraq to Indonesia and Malaysia. Terrorist attacks wrought havoc in Madrid and London.

2. Terrorism has undermined the premise of our security. National security policy has always relied on the guiding principle of deterrence between rational players. An enemy state would refrain from attacking if threatened by a counterattack sure to result in destruction or at least

defeat. This reliance on rationally calculated risk secured peace for decades between East and West. However, the global professional network of terrorism does not act according to this principle. Its calculations are not based upon this traditional sense of risk, because divine promises have been made.

In addition, terrorism is no longer the classic enemy from without. It lies both within and beyond the borders of the society under attack. Its networks are well trained, highly professional, well equipped with high-tech capabilities—and armed with a transcendence-oriented conviction that looks beyond the necessary sacrifices to a new cultural horizon.

3. Terrorism has embedded itself in many countries, effectively rescinding the traditional distinction between domestic and foreign security. Western societies, particularly the United States, have therefore replaced deterrence with the active search for protection. In recent years alone, some ninety thousand terrorists worldwide have been trained.[94] The nightmare of September 11 was, against the backdrop of this information, just the beginning of the beginning. Western civilization is facing threats to its very existence.[95]

4. Terrorism dealt the American psyche an existential blow. Attacked on its own territory, practically defenseless against an unpredictable enemy, the American nation saw the war on terrorism as necessary to ensure its own survival. The war against Iraq should not be seen as an isolated event. It is only one stone, with many more needed to complete the large mosaic of security and stability. First, there was Afghanistan, then Iraq, and other venues will follow— North Korea, Iran, Syria, Saudi Arabia, Pakistan. Wherever it sees the hint of a threat, the United States will seek to protect its national existence.

Washington would welcome the assistance of organizations such as the United Nations or NATO; but if the solidarity of international organizations does not offer help, Washington will manage on its own. The same goes for international law. When it is useful, it will be embraced; when not, America will make do without legitimation under international law. The vital interests of the security of America take priority over everything else.

94   Weidenfeld 2003b.
95   Ibid.

5. In their fundamental perceptions, their images of risk and threat, Europe and America are drifting far apart. This continental drift could lead, at some point, to a transatlantic cultural divide. To be sure, the common roots of an enlightened society, the principles of freedom and reason, have not simply withered. A close transatlantic economic relationship and social interconnection remain important.

But these are all increasingly disrupted by dissent over the use of military force, over questions of war and peace, life and death. America guaranteed its European allies a pseudo-pacifist sanctuary, which was balm to a European soul wounded by two world wars. However, when two societies respond so differently to the key challenges to their basic security, the partnership erodes, and it is only a question of time before the relationship collapses. The end of the old Atlantic community is at hand.

6. In the eyes of the rest of the world, the one remaining superpower is evidently prepared to fully realize its hegemonic status. A natural reflex in reaction to this has been a determined attempt to build temporary coalitions that relativize and curb its domination. This is the only thing that can explain the curious alliance between France, Germany, Russia and China. Within it, each partner has its own interests.

– France saw a chance to bring itself back into the circle of world powers. It is realistic enough to recognize that its strength alone is not enough. France needs partners—even if that means working with Germany, somewhat estranged of late and at best a junior partner in world political affairs.

– Germany senses the need to avert the danger of a German Sonderweg. For historical reasons, Germany requires the anchor of friendly relations more so than other nations. After having estranged itself from old partners, in particular the United States, Germany must forge new alliances. Freed from the sentimentality of the 20th century, it can ring in a new era of pragmatic partnership to assert its common interests with the United States.

– Russia is trapped in an ambivalent position. On the one hand, wounded by the loss of its superpower status, Russia seeks to benefit from a close relationship with the United States and its major market. On the other hand, too close a relationship with Washington threatens to destroy what remains of Russia's weight in world political affairs. Russia's claims of solidarity with America were a welcome diversion from domestic attention to Chechnya. However, when core elements of national pride and world political interests are at stake, Moscow knows how to define and claim its own position.

- China is the only power that could meet the United States eye to eye in the medium term. However, it needs a prudent policy that will keep its neighbors from becoming ticking time bombs through U.S. actions. The aggravation of the Indian-Pakistan conflict is one such example. This applies as well to a policy toward North Korea that could end by forcing Japan to become a nuclear power.

Considered together, all four partners share an interest in pulling away from the sole remaining superpower's magnetism, albeit for different reasons. America's hegemony is to be tamed by accumulating countervailing power.

7. America has responded to this change in the constellation with a strategy of cooperation à la carte. America's actions in waging war on Iraq have deeply divided Europe. It would be naïve to expect business as usual, to assume that the historical successes of European integration will continue. The process of European integration can also run aground; this became quite clear in the turn of events after two EU member states rejected the proposed European Constitution. The war against Iraq has given rise to basic existential questions; European states have responded by drawing on their diverse national dispositions.

Europe has no shared perception of war and peace. Each nation's own historical trauma is too different to permit such a common base. As a result, the Europeans take individual national paths, often chosen to match the contours of their relationships with the United States. This explains why Eastern and Central European states succumb to the magnetism of America's might and market. It also explains why British prime minister Tony Blair and Spain's José María Aznar sought to compensate for their limited influence in continental Europe by putting themselves shoulder to shoulder with the United States, where they could share its political spotlight and economic prospects.

A more relevant issue in the long run, however, is that trust among Europeans has been torn asunder. This became particularly clear at the June 2005 EU summit in Brussels led by EU Council

President Jean-Claude Juncker of Luxembourg. At no other summit in EU history did the different ideas of the individual nations and heads of government about the future course of the Union collide with such force. It seemed to the observer that some EU members merely had their eye on a deluxe free trade zone, while others wanted to bring the political union to completion. An even more severe problem in the wake of this summit, however, is that the assembled heads of state and government constituted not a circle of leaders energized by political courage and vision, but a bevy of relationships marked by distrust.

Considered together, these points illustrate why it is so difficult to comprehend and interpret our present situation. There are power conglomerates of a dimension heretofore unknown; societies have become more vulnerable than ever; the previous world order has given way to an anarchy of conflicts. The great dramas of human history are apparently still to be written. The reliability of our peaceful experience is a thing of the past.

What does this cultural shift mean for the transatlantic relationship? Will the cement that has held it together crumble?

The first prerequisite for a new approach is to recognize the potential of foundational models available on both sides of the Atlantic for the continuity of the Euro-American partnership. Certainly, the way Europe and the United States perceive each other includes a reservoir of friendship. Does this merely reflect the security and defense alliance they shared for 50 years, or does it spring from deeper roots, from a sense of community that will carry forward? If the latter, what dimensions of this awareness could be activated for a new and promising start?

Cooperation in security policy

Opportunities to build a new foundation for the transatlantic security alliance

The transatlantic security community is faced with new constellations of challenges on new and difficult terrain. The cohesion of its previous systems has crumbled. It must find a new direction, establish a new foundation.

The transatlantic partners after World War II faced a similar situation, one that demanded a radical paradigm shift on both sides of the Atlantic. The founders of the postwar order knew that they could not accomplish this change of course and achieve a new quality of Euro-American ties if relations within the Western community were only governed by loose arrangements. Despite the centuries of special relations between Europe and America, the gargantuan tasks of the postwar era could not have been dispatched with a handshake and a nod. The Western community needed more and better organization, which came in the form of NATO and its economic counterpart, the Marshall Plan.

The attacks on September 11, 2001, raised the same issues and challenges, but with higher stakes. In response, the Euro-American partnership must take a great step forward in terms of commitment. The key to effectively fighting international terrorism in all its forms is to rebuild the transatlantic community between the United States and the European Union on a new foundation. The first task must be to establish a clear vision of the next chapters of the transatlantic success story, unfolding under different external conditions—a vision framed as a common and ambitious goal. To that end, the new community must create an organizational framework within which its diverse and far-reaching commonalities are consolidated into a coordinated strategy for political action.

This revitalized community should thus become both catalyst and framework for the development of a contemporary agenda for all those issues no longer covered by traditional structures. This would entail not only skill in solving technical problems, but also, and more importantly, the willingness to engage in frank dialogue. Europeans and Americans alike must demonstrate unprecedented flexibility and willingness to learn. In particular, they must bid farewell to familiar and comfortable—but extremely restrictive—ways of dealing with each other, for example in discussing the sharing of international burdens.

Strategies for shaping transatlantic relations

The olden days are gone. The time has come for forward-looking strategies. Transatlantic relations are no longer geared primarily toward building a unified, free and peaceful Europe. Instead, the transatlan-

131

tic partners must meet the challenges and consequences of globalization. The United States and Europe must find common ground on which to establish a partnership for solving global problems.

Concrete plans for institutionalizing the transatlantic community can build on experiences with transnational integration in Europe and elsewhere. In view of recent challenges, action is urgently needed in the following three areas:

1. Creating effectively binding structures for consultation on economic, political and security policy across the board;
2. Overcoming limitations in trade and economic policy by setting up a transatlantic common market, exploiting good economic relationships to construct equally good security policy relationships, and developing strategies to solve the pressing problems of globalization; and
3. Exchanging experiences and information pertaining to the pressing supranational problems facing Western industrialized societies, that is, building up a transatlantic learning community.

In all of these three fields, cooperation must be governed by binding transatlantic agreements. Also needed is a robust overarching framework for the different fields of cooperation, in the form of a strategic agreement between Europe and the United States creating a transatlantic community. Whether this framework convention is established as a transatlantic contract, a charter or a binding joint declaration is of subordinate importance.

The crucial requirement is to formulate an objective that is credible for politicians and society on both sides of the Atlantic and to spell out the institutional and organizational steps to implement this objective in important fields. One example of strong cooperation along these lines is the Transatlantic Initiative for the Wider Middle East proposed by German Foreign Minister Joschka Fischer on February 6, 2004. He laid out a comprehensive plan for peace from Morocco to Israel, Palestine and Syria to Iran, Iraq and Afghanistan. The contents and the scarcity of concrete details may be disputed at length, but the approach is a step in the right direction.

To develop a new direction for common action, the transatlantic partners need a foundation that entails commitment. As early as 1990, just after the downfall of its former enemy in the east, the Western alliance already felt the need to revive cohesion within its ranks.

On November 23, 1990, immediately after the GSCE conference in Paris sanctioning the new order in Europe, the European community and the United States adopted the Transatlantic Declaration outlining the future of relations between Europe and America.

This declaration impressively affirmed the successes achieved since the war, particularly with respect to democracy, human rights and the free market economy. Committing themselves to furthering these principles throughout the world, the partners established an array of consultative mechanisms aimed at reinforcing transatlantic cooperation at all significant policy levels as well as cooperation on social issues.

Fueled by optimism stemming from success in overcoming Communism in Europe, expectations ran high that a resolute demonstration of transatlantic community spirit would suffice to advance the Western formulas for success—democracy, human rights, peaceful conflict resolution and a free market economy—all over the world.

The new world order proclaimed by then president George H. W. Bush expressed precisely this vision. In particular, he called on the states of the Western world to regard themselves, in the wake of the Cold War, as a community of global problem-solvers, charged with ridding the world of military aggression, human rights violations and economic misery once and for all. Hence, the end of the East-West conflict was seen as a major watershed. Now, all the global evil supposedly caused by this conflict could be eradicated through resolute cooperation.

A partnership at risk of erosion

The rapid Persian Gulf victory over the aggression of Saddam Hussein scored by a U.S.-led coalition in February 1991 initially seemed to stoke the optimism of the architects of the new world order. Very soon, however, it became obvious that even without the nuclear threat posed by the Warsaw Pact, the world was still a very dangerous place. The limits of Western problem-solving strategies were clearly brought to light in Somalia and Haiti between 1992 and 1994.

Likewise, more than four years of turmoil in the former Yugoslavia demonstrated the Western community's inability to prevent brutal human rights violations and aggression on its own doorstep. But it also highlighted the immense danger of such a crisis. During the Cold War, the West had planned in advance for possible aggression by the Warsaw Pact and developed structures for ending a confrontation. Without such plans and structures, the centrifugal force of a crisis could tear the West apart.

Compared with the exuberant relief of 1989/1990, then, the outlook was far more sobering. The global challenges of war, ethnically motivated atrocities, famine and terrorism proved too problematic for the West to solve in one fell swoop. The wave of domestic problems now facing America and Europe seem even more intractable. In line with logic and political realism, the concept of a new world order quietly slipped from political usage. But with it faded a common vision for an orientation to new global tasks.

At the same time, the indications have multiplied since the 1990s and particularly since the 1991 Iraq war that the traditional fabric of cooperation between Europe and America is wearing thin and threatens to dissolve completely.

The unraveling of once close-knit transatlantic relationships and the lack of a common new direction created the danger of substantial erosion, in the medium term, of the Euro-American partnership. It became painfully clear to many on both sides of the Atlantic that the Transatlantic Declaration adopted in 1990, with its ultimately nonbinding structures for cooperation, provided an inadequate foundation for truly revitalizing the transatlantic community.

Concerns persisted over the creeping erosion of the transatlantic partnership after the disappearance of the common threat. Few doubted that transatlantic cooperation needed an overhaul. Also clear was that the reconfiguration had to go beyond updating everyday political practice. The partnership needed binding structures.

Various approaches were tried, but in the absence of a clear overarching interest like that provided by security policy during the Cold War, they tended to get bogged down in the details. None of the individual areas of present-day and future cooperation, taken alone, offered a solid foundation for a revitalized transatlantic community.

The considerable pressure of political expectation ultimately resulted in the signing of two new transatlantic documents at the Euro-American summit on December 3, 1995, in Madrid. Europeans and Americans agreed on the New Transatlantic Agenda and the Joint EU/US Action Plan. In these documents, the European Union and the United States laid out in detailed and coherent form the whole spectrum of tasks they had to tackle through cooperation.

The list included restoring peace to the former Yugoslavia, stabilizing Russia's economy, creating a transatlantic economic zone and intensifying cultural cooperation. In general, the partners made a commitment to coordinate their efforts to support peace, stability, democracy and economic development all over the world. With regard to bilateral trade, they agreed to conduct a joint study aimed at finding ways to reduce trade barriers. Furthermore, the documents identified a number of specific economic topics (such as cooperation between customs authorities) where efforts would be made to conclude bilateral agreements in the near future.

Critics of reconfiguring transatlantic structures argue that new forms of binding cooperation between Europe and America have not yet found their way onto the agenda primarily because transatlantic commonalities narrowed after the Cold War ended. In their view, new levels of commitment are voluntarist; in particular, they place too heavy a burden on existing structures and thus contribute to their disintegration.

Does this mean that efforts to revitalize the transatlantic community on a new foundation spring from an outdated illusion of harmony? On the contrary: Closer scrutiny of the critics' arguments reveals that nearly all their objections to new structures of coordination focus on individual aspects of the new models and deplore their lack of feasibility and/or their detrimental effect on Euro-American relations. In most cases, this criticism does not penetrate to the core of the current discussion, namely the objective interest in and need for a new common approach to political, economic and social issues on both sides of the Atlantic. Beyond the individual proposals under discussion at the moment, what is the basis for this need?

Lines of conflict between the United States and Europe

The answer can be found in closer analysis of the lines of conflict between Europeans and Americans. It is true that when the transatlantic partners attempt to solve international crises, differences—and sometimes quite spectacular ones—have often come to light. The contrasting views of a second military intervention in Iraq illustrated

135

this yet again. Before and during the 2003 Iraq war, domestic political calculations, coupled with a mixture of mental distance and differences within Europe, laid bare an extremely ambivalent relationship between Europe and the United States. However, it is also true that in almost every international crisis, the Europeans and Americans are capable of working toward a common aim against a common adversary. Often, they and they alone can secure and implement constructive solutions.

Nonetheless cause for concern is the fact that Americans and Europeans have not yet arrived at a common strategic assessment of the global political situation. After September 11, 2001, the United States pursued its own strategic mission to protect itself and to preserve its status as a world power. Meanwhile, the absence of a common strategic culture in Europe represents the Achilles heel of European foreign policy. The global political situation, however, demands a joint effort by Americans and Europeans in a strategic community. Therefore, the primary goal must be to take advantage of this crisis in the transatlantic relationship, gleaning every possible lesson that can further the cause of solving the global problem of terrorism, its causes and its consequences.

During the period of East-West confrontation, all partners could count on the common security policy as a given. Today, as we seek to reestablish the transatlantic community, we have no single overarching principle to rely on. Therefore, our efforts to establish new binding structures or to adapt existing ones must center on issues where the partners have an obvious and paramount interest in joint action.

In view of the focal points of European and American political activity, the greatest need lies in coordinating strategies to respond to global challenges or international crises. Nowadays, Europe and the United States are the only reliable producers or guarantors of stability in the world. Given the number and variety of international hot spots, the transatlantic partners must respond to calls for assistance almost on a daily basis—and often in regions and areas where the institutions of the North Atlantic alliance have no jurisdiction. There is, as yet, no permanent coordination mechanism between Europe and the United States to deal with these issues. Now that the traditional security partnership has been somewhat watered down, however, there is an increasingly real danger that these conflicts will exert their centrifugal forces within the transatlantic community as well. What is more, this development must be seen against the backdrop of ever-greater absorption with domestic challenges both in the United States and in the EU member states.

Pragmatic cooperation

Therefore, it is vital to set up a binding structure for transatlantic political consultation that would give the transatlantic partners a reliable mandate to coordinate all issues that are relevant to the transatlantic agenda. It is high time for the transatlantic community to create such a mechanism—to establish a Euro-American Political Cooperation (EAPC). This EAPC would offer a timely forum for dealing with all the issues that the international community directs at the transatlantic partners but that are not yet accommodated in any organizational form. Pressing topics falling under the domain of this forum for political coordination could include the coordination of common transatlantic strategies for tackling the main international challenges of the day—particularly in waging the war against global terrorism, but also in bringing about a peaceful solution in the Middle East or developing strategies to combat global environmental destruction.

Euro-American Political Cooperation would have to extend to all multilateral forums—the United Nations, disarmament conferences, the World Trade Organization and others. All these organizations would have to establish transatlantic consultation groups, as has been the practice for coordination within Europe for some time now.

The New Transatlantic Agenda adopted in Madrid on December 3, 1995, contains a well-structured catalog of topics for joint political consultation. All pressing issues facing the transatlantic partners are listed as objects of Euro-American coordination efforts. This impressive agenda offers further evidence of the urgent need to introduce the binding structures that would allow this coordination. The institution of Euro-American Political Cooperation would achieve just that.

This approach has been discussed under a variety of headings. One example is the concept of a G-2 caucus, in which the European Union and the United States would establish close cooperation and thus advance the transatlantic agenda. In their capacity as leading nations, they would tackle global problems and develop strategies to solve them. The initiators of this concept assume that the economic relationships, which are functioning well, can and must have a positive effect on the security relationships, which are not functioning so well. This approach would not only revitalize the transatlantic partnership, but also attempt to solve the problems at the international level caused by globalization.[96]

NATO—relic or key to a fresh start?

Division of tasks between the EU and NATO as a model for the future

Thus, before transatlantic relations took on new forms after World War II, the states of Europe and the United States already possessed a rich history of common political activity and economic independence. On both sides of the Atlantic, the awareness was firmly rooted that strategies for solving international problems had a chance of success only in cooperation with the transatlantic partner.

At the time, however, the founding of the Western alliance—primarily NATO—as well as its economic correlate in Europe, the EEC, was anything but obvious. The numerous political disputes, especially within the European countries, made this plain. Only because these new structures worked well during the postwar period and the time of the Cold War can we now regard them as the only possible outcome of World War II.

The division of tasks between the EU and NATO will take center stage during the 21st century. Though the world was unprepared for the September 11 attacks, it had long recognized terrorism as a threat to international security and stability. Even in the 1990s, there was consensus that international terrorism posed a multifaceted threat. But there were no specific common ideas about how to address this threat. In earlier decades, the threat from an imperialist ideology embodied in Soviet power structures had united the transatlantic community and held together its institutionalized form, NATO. When the Soviet Union fell, that conceptual cement also crumbled.

"NATO, once the most important institution for balancing transatlantic interests in security matters, has practically fallen by the way-

---

96 For more on the G-2 approach, see Weidenfeld et al. 2004.

side."[97] Thomas Risse's assessment need not stand; the EU on one side of the Atlantic and the United States on the other could counteract it. NATO has added seven member states—impressive evidence that these two partners have not yet completely written off the security alliance. The new EU members also rely more on NATO's shield than on the EU Security and Defense Policy; they view the United States as the victor in the Cold War, the power that won their freedom.[98]

What does it mean not to have fully written off an institution? It means that both partners regard reorganization and a new assignment of tasks as within the realm of possibility. They already agree that the NATO mandate quite clearly extends beyond Europe's borders and that NATO's new Response Force might soon have to intervene outside Europe. Underpinning this Response Force is the concurrence between France and Great Britain. In their summit meeting on November 24, 2002, they committed themselves to improving relations between the EU and NATO and to enhancing interoperability between the EU rapid intervention troops and the NATO Response Force. Hence, at least in the first decade of the new century—and despite the potential for consternation on all sides—coalitions of the willing could certainly play a role within NATO; not all European states are equally prepared for military engagement.

Differing assessments of military potentials

One obvious transatlantic problem in the framework of NATO is the capabilities gap dramatically revealed during the Kosovo intervention and confirmed in Afghanistan. In 2002, the United States spent more than twice as much on defense ($335 billion) as the 15 EU member states combined ($153 billion).[99] In such a situation, it is probably only normal for the United States to categorize Europe's development of its own capabilities as duplication at the expense of NATO. But on closer scrutiny, the requirements set forth in the EU headline goals turn out to be entirely compatible with those of NATO's Defense

97 Risse 2003, 15.
98 Samson 2003
99 Sipri Yearbook 2003, Appendix 10 A, Table 10A.1 (data on the EU) and Table 10A.3 (data on the United States).

Capabilities Initiative. In fact, the harmonization of capacities within Europe can only help. Here too, the key to a higher level of interoperability lies in closer cooperation between the European and American arms industries, which could even initiate military specifications.

In addition to this capabilities gap, the two partners' different conceptual approaches to the role of military power in international relations also have major significance. Robert Kagan launched this discussion when he determined that the Europeans had turned away from power and maintained that the United States exercises power in a world "where international laws and rules are unreliable and where true security and the defense and promotion of a liberal order still depend on the possession and use of military might."[100]

In fact, however, the United States overestimates the capabilities of military power, as the derailed peace process in Iraq and the terrorist attacks in Madrid and London have sadly borne out. The military superiority of the United States does not suffice to establish peace and order at a global level. At the same time, the Europeans underestimate the relevance of force as a thorny issue in international relations. For both partners, cooperation in an organization such as NATO can lay the groundwork for rethinking their respective analyses of the global situation and arriving at a new strategy together. If NATO did not exist, we would need to invent it.

Economic cooperation and rivalry within the WTO

The United States and the EU in the context of global economic relations

In addition to security policy, it is also useful to look at the attitudes of the United States and the EU as global trading partners—especially at the shaping of their economic relationships, their potential influence on international trade and the potential for conflict.

---

100 Kagan 2003, 7.

As long as protectionist tendencies dominate in many nations, world trade will never reach its full potential for growth and prosperity—so goes the credo of the World Trade Organization (WTO). The WTO aims to dismantle trade barriers and thereby realize gains for all involved—poor countries and rich alike. For example, the World Bank has estimated that implementing the Doha Development Agenda (DDA), launched in 2001 in Qatar, could raise global earnings by $500 billion per year by 2015, with 60 percent of this increase going to developing nations.[101] That now seems unlikely—the breakdown of the Cancún ministerial conference was enough to scuttle the timeline set in Doha.

The failure of WTO talks in Cancún highlighted one fact: Faced with intractable national interests, compromise has no chance. The rifts that must be bridged within the WTO are wide, as the political dealings of the United States and the EU in that institution make plain.

As close bilateral trade partners, the United States and the EU constitute the largest trade blocks within the WTO. Although Asia and the Pacific rim have gained importance for the United States, the EU remains its most significant trade partner—and vice versa. In 2003, EU exports to the United States amounted to 208 billion (35 percent of all EU exports); imports from the United States totaled 151 billion (22 percent of all EU imports).[102] In turn, the United States in 2003 exported to the EU goods valued at $149 billion (21 percent of all U.S. exports) and imported goods valued at $245 billion (19 percent of all imports).[103]

Approximately one third of transatlantic trade takes place between European or U.S. corporations and their subsidiaries. This corporate structure also functions as a natural buffer against protectionism, since transatlantic groups are less interested in trade protection against

---

101 World Bank Group 2004, 144.
102 Hamilton/Quinlan 2004, 173.
103 Office of the U.S. Trade Representative: 2004 National Trade Estimate Report European Union, www.ustr.gov/assets/World_Regions/Europe_Mediterranean/European_Union/asset_upload_file510_4193.pdf, 1 (accessed January 1, 2005).

companies within their group and set much greater store by open trade and investment arrangements on both sides of the Atlantic.[104]

In view of these figures, it comes as no surprise that more than half the foreign earnings of American companies originate in Europe. Likewise, the sum earned in the United States by multinational European companies has risen to $46 billion. Although total trade between the United States and Asia is approximately 50 percent higher than total transatlantic trade, the United States and the EU constitute by far the largest bilateral trade relationship in the world.

The centerpiece of transatlantic trade is not trade in goods. Far more important are investments, which—in both directions combined—amounted to 1.5 trillion in 2003.[105] Despite all political tensions, EU citizens in 2003 invested around 889 billion in the United States, while U.S. citizens invested 650 billion in the EU—a sum that amounted to 65 percent of all U.S. foreign investments.[106]

The two trade partners have also posted impressive figures reflecting the effect of their economic interconnectedness on employment. In 2001, 3.2 million Europeans worked for U.S. companies; that represents 43 percent of all foreign employees of U.S. companies. In the same year, European companies in the United States employed more than 4.2 million workers.[107]

Furthermore, the good economic relations between the United States and the EU also profited from trade with the new EU member states. The elimination of national customs duties for the countries of Southern and Eastern Europe, along with the general lowering of customs tariffs from an average of nine percent to four percent, promises advantages for trade with third countries. For U.S. companies, investment sites in Central and Eastern Europe are becoming cost-effective portals to markets within Europe. The harmonization of statutes and regulations further facilitates trade. U.S. exports into the region more than doubled between 1990 and 2001, and it seems likely that the flow of trade will continue to expand. As in the rest of Europe, U.S. investments will gain importance here; for example, U.S. subsidiaries

104 Schott/Hufbauer 2003, 1.
105 European Commission: European Union Factsheet: EU-US Bilateral Economic Relations, http://trade-info.cec.eu.int/doclib/docs/2003/october/tradoc_114064.pdf, 2 (accessed January 1, 2005).
106 Hamilton/Quinlan 2004, 138ff.
107 Ibid.

increased their earnings from $500 million in 1990 to $35 billion in 2001.[108]

Steps to liberalize world trade

While these long-term and stable flows of trade are supported by bilateral agreements such as the New Transatlantic Agenda and the Transatlantic Economic Partnership, the WTO has apparently been relegated to the role of conflict mediator in this busy twosome. The coordination of trade policy has certainly improved since the organization was founded, but the high expectations for transatlantic relations associated with this institution have not been met.[109]

The increasing trend toward the regionalization of U.S. trade policy,[110] the persistently protectionist policies of the EU and the United States, and the WTO's failures—greeted by some observers with a touch of spite—raise the question of whether cooperation between the EU and the United States within the WTO can ever go beyond lip service, and hence whether the WTO can ever constitute an appropriate forum for setting the transatlantic community on a new footing.

The basis for any cooperation between the United States and the EU in the WTO is their fundamental commitment to supporting and expanding the multilateral trade system.[111]

Few problems arise when it comes to formulating general intermediate objectives—such as implementing agreements within the framework of the WTO; further opening markets, especially for services; holding multilateral negotiations to advance reforms in the agricultural sector in full compliance with WTO regulations; and intensifying efforts within the WTO. Before talks opened in Doha, the EU and the United States agreed on two common positions that—details aside—would determine the common basic direction of their negotiations. Both support sustainable development; both regard strengthening global trade as an indispensable weapon in fighting poverty.

108 Ibid.
109 Krell 2003, 26.
110 Gordon 2003, 105–118.
111 European Commission: Trade Issues: Bilateral Trade Relations: USA, www.europa. eu.int/comm/trade/issues/bilateral/countries/usa/index_en.htm (accessed January 1, 2005).

Beneath the overarching goal of liberalizing global trade, ideas on how to reach this goal differ.[112] While the EU often gives the impression that it wants to widen the scope of work of the WTO, the United States seems to focus on intensifying its work—that is, within the framework of existing regulations, it evidently seeks to dismantle barriers in order to achieve unlimited access in key markets.

By contrast, the EU's approach must be viewed through the lens of its experiences with European integration. Its goal is to establish a supranational system, a sort of economic government that would control advancing globalization. One way to do that is to bring more areas, such as environmental protection, under a comprehensive regulatory system.

The rocky path to multilateral consensus

Over the course of half a century, successive rounds of multilateral negotiations—including the Kennedy, Tokyo and Uruguay rounds—have altered the landscape of global trade. Negotiators lowered tariffs and other trade barriers and, in 1994, created the WTO—the successor to the General Agreement on Tariffs and Trade (GATT)—as a permanent forum for trade negotiations and a body that could rule on disputes arising from practice of the resolutions. But the 1999 attempt to launch a new trade round in Seattle ended in disaster. The problems at the conference went beyond the inability of rich and poor countries to reach a compromise on further trade liberalization. The massive and even violent protests by opponents of globalization also cast a shadow on the WTO's work.

Even before the start of negotiations in Doha in November 2001, it was clear that the spectacle could not be repeated. Officials at WTO headquarters in Geneva agreed that if the Doha talks failed, multilateral trade negotiations would "go into hibernation." In an increasingly interconnected world, any bilateral and regional talks occurring in their place would cost developing countries dearly.[113]

---

112 Zoellick 2002, 26.
113 The Economist: Playing games with prosperity, July 26, 2001, www.economist. com/displaystory.cfm?story_id=709533

Thus, the pressure lay on the United States and the EU, the two biggest players, to make sure the Doha negotiations succeeded. Granted, their cooperation could not guarantee success, but it made it more likely. Six topics were on the agenda: agriculture, the environment, anti-dumping laws, implementation of the agreements reached in the Uruguay round, intellectual property rights, and investment and competition policies.

Those meeting in advance of the conference had their work cut out for them. In the area of agriculture, where the EU drew fire chiefly because of its high subsidies, and in their recommendations to improve global environmental protection, the Europeans could expect to find little favor with the United States. Conversely, U.S. interests came under pressure on anti-dumping laws and intellectual property rights, the latter in part because developing countries were being denied access to effective and affordable prescription drugs.

Despite the huge significance of the trade round, the two principals could not arrive at an advance agreement that would signal a breakthrough. Their top two negotiators, EU trade commissioner Pascal Lamy and U.S. trade representative Robert Zoellick, had worked closely together for the past five years, but the sole result before the actual negotiations began was a draft hammered out with other participants that merely restated known positions.

The talks held in Doha on November 9–14, 2001, laid the groundwork for the Doha Development Agenda, whose object was to strengthen the multilateral trade system in areas such as agriculture and industry. According to the timeline established there, further negotiations would be completed no later than January 1, 2005. But after the September 2003 ministerial conference in Cancún ran aground, the schedule had to be extended. In view of the difficult battles waged, the agreements that were reached in Doha—for example, on reducing farm subsidies, on relaxing intellectual property rights to benefit developing countries, and on dealing with additional violations in anti-dumping laws—must be considered an achievement.

The goal of the ministerial conference in Cancún was to take stock of the Doha process and, by demonstrating leadership and resolve, to lay the groundwork for more productive decision-making.[114]

114 World Trade Organization 2001.

Transatlantic trade conflicts and possible solutions

Transatlantic trade disputes

In contrast to Doha, the runup to the ministerial conference in Cancún featured relatively close cooperation—particularly in the agricultural sector—between the EU and the United States. Going into the conference, their positions had been on a collision course. In July 2002, the United States was still calling for radical reform of subsidies and tariffs, while the European response in December 2002 sought merely to take up where the limited results of the Uruguay round had left off. The measures proposed by the United States would have come chiefly at the expense of the EU and Japan; the EU plans for revaluating government subsidies would have required reforms particularly in the United States.[115]

In the end, however, a signal came that the two parties had found their way back to cooperation. They issued a joint paper on the agricultural sector, the substance of which rested chiefly on three pillars: steps to deal with national subsidies, comprehensive access to markets and export competition. As it turned out, these talking points amounted to little more than a selection of problem areas; many other points required further negotiation.[116]

Nevertheless, the draft of a joint position provided a blueprint—even if details and future obligations were for the most part excluded.

Substantively, the paper offered little that was new. It proposed decisive cutbacks in national assistance and subsidies. With regard to market access, it both acknowledged the value opening it up comprehensively, and took into consideration the protection of sensitive products. This point mattered a great deal especially to developing countries, which need to be able to protect their goods against cheaper imports. With regard to export competition, the EU and the United States managed to agree on a list of products for which subsidies should be lifted at once to benefit the developing countries.

Even as an official document, the paper was intended only to provide input and give new impetus to the negotiations; therefore, this

---

115 Schott/Hufbauer 2003, 3.
116 European Commission: Sectoral Issues: Trade in agricultural goods and fishery products, from 13.08.03, www.europa.eu.int/comm/trade/issues/sectoral/agri_fish/pr140803_en.htm (accessed January 13, 2005).

initiative must not be overrated. Despite initial euphoria on the part of the European and U.S. participants, they could not reach agreement with the other 144 states. The implication is quite clear: Even if the two largest trade blocs demonstrate unity, successful negotiations in the WTO are far from guaranteed.

Not to be overlooked here is one important aspect of the political negotiations that causes a good deal of tension in the transatlantic relationship and leads to rivalry instead of cooperation. In their negotiations on further trade liberalization, each side skillfully stakes out its own positions—at the expense of its transatlantic partner. The EU and the United States each take pains to portray the other side as tight-fisted, in order to secure for themselves the support of developing nations. This behavior is particularly evident in the high-profile areas of agricultural trade (to include genetic engineering) and pharmaceuticals. So far, however, this rivalry has cropped up at the periphery of transatlantic economic relations, not at the center.[117]

Although both sides generally make an effort to reach bilateral settlements, many contacts between the United States and the EU occur before the Dispute Settlement Body, the WTO's arbitration committee. Particularly extensive in recent years have been disputes over genetically modified organisms (GMOs) and U.S. legislation in support of exporters.

The revolution in biotechnology in the past decade opened new horizons for production and trade, but it also revealed a new dimension for concerns about its long-term effects on human health and the environment. Opinions differ particularly in the debate over GMOs, which have not yet been proven to be either dangerous or safe. As a consequence of this uncertainty, some governments have banned them outright, striking just the right nerve among the public—at least in Europe. Because the justification for this defensive stance is that it aims to protect the population, there can be little argument against what many in the United States view as a European wave of protectionism.

Unlike hormone-treated foods, GMOs are not totally prohibited in Europe. But they arouse more concern among the European public than in the United States. As a result, the European Commission long refrained from lifting its 1999 moratorium on the sale of GMOs.

117 Schott/Hufbauer 2003, 2.

Imports of genetically modified grain from the United States are prohibited; other products still await approval for importation into the European market.

In view of these trade barriers, the United States brought a suit before the WTO. As a result, the EU had to lift the moratorium and resort to legislation. As of April 18, 2004, genetically modified food and feed are subject to regulation (EC) No. 1829/2003. The regulation sets forth a uniform procedure within the European Community for the approval of all food and feed obtained from GMOs. In addition, the rules require labeling for all genetically modified seed—a stipulation that led the United States to file another complaint before the WTO.

Another dispute that the EU and the United States sought to clarify within the WTO concerns what are known as foreign sales corporations.[118] A U.S. law that took effect in 1984 allowed exporters to exempt from taxable income a portion of their export profits. In 1998, the EU filed a complaint, arguing that such tax exemptions represented hidden export subsidies that violated WTO regulations.

In October 1999, the WTO ruled in favor of the EU. The United States was told to revise its tax code to comply with WTO regulations by the year 2000. If it failed to do so, the EU would have the right to institute penalties in the amount of $4 billion per year. However, the EU Commission was not primarily interested in retaliatory measures; it mainly wanted the United States to cease export subsidies in violation of WTO regulations.[119] To avoid the penalties, the United States replaced the original legislation with the Extraterritorial Income (ETI) Exclusion Act[120]. But because that too provided subsidies for exporters, the WTO rejected it in January 2002.

Faced with continued noncompliance of the U.S. law with WTO regulations, the EU on March 1, 2004, levied an additional customs duty of 5 percent on selected U.S. products, with automatic monthly increases by 1 percent until the duty reached a maximum of 17 per-

118 Ahearn 2003, 6.
119 European Commission: External Trade: WTO Dispute Settlement, What's New?, vom 13.9.02, www.europa.eu.int/comm/trade/miti/dispute/pr130902_de.htm (accessed January 1, 2005).
120 European Commission: European Union: Factsheet: US Non-Compliance with WTO Rulings, http://trade-info.cec.eu.int/doclib/docs/2003/october/tradoc_114065.pdf, 2 (accessed January 1, 2005).

cent on March 1, 2005. Any additional countermeasures have not yet been established.[121] On February 13, the WTO appellate body ruled that US tax subsidies for exporters were in breach of the WTO's rules. The EU is currently threatening with "retaliatory measures" if the US fails to comply with the ruling.[122]

Yet another example of the strategic rivalry between Europe and the United States concerned subsidies for the European aircraft manufacturer Airbus and that corporation's success. The dispute flared when U.S. trade representative Robert Zoellick informed the EU that Washington had wearied of efforts to talk the EU out of the unfair billions in subsidies. The Europeans in turn accused the United States of massive illegal subsidies for the U.S. giant Boeing and called the U.S. suit a diversionary tactic. The U.S. government, viewing the Airbus subsidies as an infringement of international trade law, sought WTO arbitration at the end of 2004. The WTO has formed an arbitration panel that must rule on the Airbus subsidies by early 2006.

Initiatives for resolving transatlantic trade disputes

A variety of approaches to curbing such disputes have emerged over the years. In the 1995 New Transatlantic Agenda, the United States and the EU made a commitment to strengthen multilateral trade and to establish a transatlantic marketplace by progressively reducing or eliminating trade and investment barriers. One outcome of this shared agenda was the Transatlantic Business Dialogue (TABD), which has been somewhat sidelined in recent years but otherwise survived the transatlantic rifts largely unscathed. This dialogue among company CEOs and business leaders also paved the way for the Transatlantic Economic Partnership inaugurated in 1998, which addressed important aspects of bilateral and multilateral trade and capital markets.

While these initiatives pay dividends for transatlantic relations, they cannot uphold the partnership over the long haul without a corresponding commitment to good relations at the highest political level. Nor can

---

121 European Commission: Trade Issues: Respecting the Rules: WTO Dispute Settlement vom 27.2.04, www.europa.eu.int/comm/trade/issues/respectrules/dispute/pr270204_en.htm (accessed January 13, 2005).

122 "WTO ruling on tax subsidies sparks EU/US trade flare-up", 14.02.06, www.euractive.com (accessed February 15, 2006)

personal friendships among the political elite provide a durable foundation for an Atlantic partnership.[123] In addition, many of these transatlantic initiatives have fizzled after just a few years, while transatlantic squabbles like the ones before the WTO stay in the public eye.

On a purely factual basis, bilateral economic relations remain the driving force in the transatlantic relationship despite the simmering trade disputes.[124] No more than five percent of bilateral transatlantic trade is even affected by the trade conflicts. Hence, trade wars or other major conflicts that might seriously threaten economic relations appear unlikely.[125]

But within the WTO, hard facts are not all that matter. Other factors that influence its decisions have negative repercussions when it comes to cooperation between the United States and the EU. It is no secret that the two partners are at odds about the importance of international organizations and hence of the WTO itself.[126] In Europe, there is strong support for the primacy of international law and its institutions, which are regarded as having intrinsic value. In the United States, international obligations are traditionally balanced against national interests and generally held suspect out of concern for national sovereignty.

To make matters worse, the WTO summits draw worldwide media attention that downright encourages political rhetoric. Furthermore, the principle of unanimity has not changed since the GATT took effect—but the number of members has climbed from 84 (in 1979) to 147 (in 2004).[127] Channels for organizing interests are sparse, increasing the tendency to go it alone. Those who dig in their heels earn bonus points at home; holding the line can often bear more fruit than sustained efforts to liberalize world trade. The complexity of the decision-making process makes it difficult to sort out responsibility for what happens or to assign concrete blame when negotiations break down, as in Cancún.

Because of these ideological differences and the WTO's structural deficits, cooperation between the United States and the EU in that institution is severely limited, making it ill suited to become a new

123 Steinberg 2003, 259.
124 Linn 2004b, 2.
125 European Economic Group CESifo 2004.
126 Rubenfeld 2004, 3.
127 Schott 2000.

pillar of transatlantic relations. Over the years, the United States and the EU settled on an informal modus operandi in their bilateral trade cooperation and their activity in multilateral economic forums—one that essentially relied on the cordial relationship between Robert Zoellick and Pascal Lamy, who no longer have responsibility for trade negotiations.

Efforts to build a durable foundation

But personal relationships of that nature likewise cannot serve as the durable foundation for transatlantic economic relations. Nor has a comparable connection ever existed between the U.S. Justice Department's antitrust division and the EU competition commission. Otherwise, transatlantic tensions might not have run so high in 2001 when the EU Commission blocked the merger of U.S. conglomerates General Electric and Honeywell, or in the EU's long-running cartel case against Microsoft.

One alternative—a key recommendation from a strategy group on economics, finance and trade—is an institutionalized G-2 approach. A G-2 caucus would sort out transatlantic issues before they reached the G-7 or G-8 level. Possible topics for dialogue include competition policy, integration of financial markets and macroeconomic cooperation, but also more general fields such as energy policy, environmental policy and migration.[128]

Two primary insights from the political arena also apply in the economic arena when it comes to the prerequisites for a vital transatlantic community: Europe must remedy its strategic deficits, both conceptual and structural; it still focuses too much on reaching consensus, still makes too little effort to project its power. The United States must take heed that no single power acting on its own can make a permanent mark on international politics. Both must recognize that strength exerts an enduring influence when it does not stand alone.

The overarching aim must be to build a strategic community to address important transatlantic—but also global—issues in economics and finance. In the past, despite foreign policy crises, economic cooperation between the United States and the EU has generally

128 For a full discussion, see Weidenfeld et. al. 2004.

remained stable, so that economics was a function of security. The converse could apply today: A new security relationship could be a function of economics. That is, problems on the security side could be tackled through closer cooperation in economics, finance and trade in a G-2 network. The strategic gain lies in the fact that such a G-2 caucus would operate as an informal steering group, not a new bureaucracy or new institution and not a replacement for mechanisms that already exist, whether the G-7 or other multilateral forums. The G-2 would supplement these with a forum in which the two transatlantic partners, the United States and the EU, could agree on critical issues in advance and take a position of leadership together, as individuals such as Lamy and Zoellick have done with good results.

The fundamental thesis is that these two economic heavyweights must join forces as never before to exercise global leadership on important matters. Of course, this also raises two crucial political questions: Who speaks for Europe? And can the United States act other than unilaterally?

Cultural cooperation

Alongside the transatlantic bonds forged by decades of political and economic cooperation are cultural bridges that stand on solid footing on both continents. The list is long and diverse: American cultural institutes in Europe and their counterparts in the United States, the European Union Centers; exchange programs at high schools, colleges and universities; sister-city pairings; and private foundations and associations with a transatlantic reach. All primarily aim to promote transatlantic understanding in civil society and to secure future cooperation by broadening contacts not only between government officials but among individuals from of all walks of life.

The value of these civilian contacts was also reflected in the New Transatlantic Agenda and the Joint EU/US Action Plan inaugurated by the EU and the United States at their 1995 summit in Madrid.[129]

---

129 European Commission: The EU's relations with the United States of America. Joint EU–US Action Plan, IV. Building Bridges Across the Atlantic, www.europa. eu.int/comm/external_relations/us/action_plan/4_building_bridges.htm (accessed January 13, 2005).

Their representatives laid out for the first time a detailed and coherent spectrum of security, stability and global challenges that they agreed to tackle together. At the same time, they paid tribute to their populations' contribution to good transatlantic relations.

"We recognize that the transatlantic relationship can be truly secure in the coming century only if future generations understand its importance as well as their parents and grandparents did. We are committed to fostering an active and vibrant transatlantic community by deepening and broadening the commercial, social, cultural, scientific, and educational ties that bind us,"[130] the declaration stated. Under the heading of Building Bridges Across the Atlantic, the signatories pledged to advance the Transatlantic Business Dialogue and broaden cooperation in science and technology, but also to improve people-to-people links with a view to making intellectual and personal transatlantic exchanges as profitable as possible for both sides.

For cultural ties to thrive, they must be deeply rooted in an open willingness to understand another society and other views. Cultural cooperation carries particular importance because it takes a long-term perspective and because its outcomes have strong political implications. Cities do not terminate their partnerships overnight in response to political discord; yearlong cultural exchanges generally inoculate their participants against opportunistic anti-Americanism and foster the vital habits of international understanding.

But the converse is also true: Without a sufficient commitment to cultural relations, they can begin to erode. The extent of the damage may not come to light until difficulties can no longer be resolved using old patterns and models. The traditional ties across the Atlantic remain largely intact; a cultural split is not imminent. And yet—in part because of Europeans' unfavorable reaction to recent U.S. foreign policy decisions[131]—the danger cannot simply be dismissed.

130 Ibid., 1.
131 Poll by Chicago Council on Foreign Relations and German Marshall Funds of the United States Worldviews 2002: Europeans see the world as Americans do, but critical of U.S. foreign policy, www.worldviews.org/docs/TransatlanticKeyFind ings.pdf (accessed January 13, 2005), 3 f.

First conceived soon after World War I, the idea of linking cities and towns across the Atlantic was revived after World War II as a way to promote international reconciliation. Over the years, the first initiatives[132] grew into organized and institutionalized programs that included some 170 partnerships within German-American relations alone.[133] Since 2001, EU grants for city partnerships have risen from 10 million to 12 million, and the number of projects supported has grown from 955 to 1,328.[134] The declared goal is to promote an active European civil society.[135] The U.S. government also provides support, but the total funding is difficult to determine because subsidies are posted under different budget items.

The largest American organization to specialize in linking partner cities and towns is Sister Cities International. Dating back to an initiative of President Eisenhower in 1956, the organization aims to reduce the chance of future world conflict by nurturing and promoting citizen diplomacy within the framework of partnerships. Nowadays, Japan and Germany account for the largest number of U.S. partner cities, organized in a network of coordinators, committees and volunteers. Sister Cities International is financed mostly through contributions from the member cities, which range from \$130 to \$1200 per year, depending on the city's size.[136] Thus, city partnerships represent a small but steady and successful component of transatlantic relationships.

Federal states across the Atlantic have also paired up. In Germany alone, four states maintain relationships with sister states in the United States (Bavaria with California, Brandenburg and Rhineland–

---

132 The first city partnerships included Crailsheim and Worthington, Minn., and Ludwigshafen and Pasadena, Cal. in 1947.

133 Homepage: The U.S. Diplomatic Mission to Germany: Deutsch–Amerikanische Städtepartnerschaften, http://usembassy.state.gov/germany/sistercities.html (accessed January 13, 2005).

134 European Commission: City partnerships: Number of applications submitted from 2001 to 2003, 08/04, www.europa. eu.int/comm/dgs/education_culture/towntwin/doc/projects01_en.pdf (accessed January 13, 2005).

135 European Council decision on an EC Action Plan to promote an active European civil society, in: Amtsblatt der Europäischen Union L30 vom 4.2.2004, 6–14.

136 For details, see The U.S. Diplomatic Mission to Germany: Sister Cities, http://usembassy.state.gov/germany/sistercities.html (accessed January 13, 2005), und Sister Cities International, www.sister-cities.org/ (accessed January 13, 2005).

Palatinate with South Carolina, Hessen with Wisconsin), though only the relationship between Hessen and Wisconsin is based on a formal contract.

Cooperation in higher education

Exchange programs for students and young academics play a special role as part of cultural cooperation between the EU and the United States. In the long run, good transatlantic relationships can be kept alive only if sensitivity to other ways of thinking and ways of life, and the awareness that they can profit from these relationships is firmly anchored in the younger generations. The many established exchange programs aim to foster these attitudes.

The most important of these is the EU–US Cooperation Programme in Higher Education and Vocational Education Training, which in 2000 was extended to 2005.[137] The program aims to promote understanding, improve the quality of human resource development and engender new forms of cooperation between the United States and the EU. In each of the 25 EU member states, it sets out to develop a consortium of at least three EU institutions and three U.S. institutions that may also work with local chambers of commerce, nongovernmental organizations and businesses. The program gains stature by cooperating with the Fulbright Foundation, one of the most important U.S. institutions for university exchange programs. Between 1995 and 2000, the program established 53 transatlantic consortia in which more than 400 European and American institutions and some 4,000 students participated.

In addition to this officially institutionalized cooperation, school and student exchanges constitute an important cultural and social bridge between the two continents. In the academic year 2003/2004 alone, around 74,400 European students studied in the United States; in the same year, some 110,000 U.S. students attended European higher educational institutions. The European country sending the greatest number of students to the United States was Turkey (2003/

137 European Commission: Education and Training: Programs and Actions: EU-USA: The EU-US Cooperation Programme in Higher Education and Vocational Education Training 2001–2005, www.europa.eu.int/comm/education/programmes/eu-usa/index_en.html (accessed January 13, 2005).

2004: 11,400 students, 8th place), followed by Germany (8,700 students, 11th place), Great Britain (8,400 students, 12th place) and France (6,800 students, 18th place). By way of comparison: India (79,700 students) and China (61,800 students) held first and second place.

In the opposite direction, Europe clearly held top rank for U.S. students abroad. Led by Great Britain, which in 2002/2003 hosted 31,700 U.S. students, followed by Spain and Italy (18,900 each), France (13,100), Germany (5,600) and Ireland (4,900), six European nations ranked among the top ten destinations for U.S. students abroad. Percentage-wise, however, Europe lost importance for U.S. university exchange programs, though it held on to its unchallenged top ranking. While in the 1985/86 school year 80 percent of all U.S. visiting students traveled to Europe, this percentage steadily declined to 63 percent in 2002/2003; by contrast, Latin America increased its share from 7 to 15 percent and Oceania's share rose from 1 to 7 percent.[138]

An often-underestimated problem in academic cooperation between the EU and the United States is the ongoing brain drain—the migration of highly qualified academics. The United States has been one of the greatest magnets for foreign researchers. Approximately 15 percent of the doctorate recipients in the United States are Europeans; approximately three-fourths of them remain in the United States and enter the U.S. job market—compared with 49 percent in 1990.[139]

The attractiveness of the U.S. research and job market is primarily responsible for this emigration. In May 2004, approximately 970,000 researchers were working in the European Union. After its expansion, some 110,000 researchers in the 10 acceding countries joined their ranks, but the total was still approximately 175,000 lower than in the United States.

Approximately 50 percent of scientists in the pre-expansion EU held jobs in the private sector (significantly less in the acceding countries); the corresponding figure for the United States stood at approximately 80 percent. Even the European Commission sees this sustained brain drain from Europe toward North America as a danger.

---

138 All data from Institute for International Education, http://opendoors.iienetwork.org.
139 European Commission 2003, 23.

Indeed, the United States recruits some two percent of its researchers in Europe.[140]

After September 11, 2001, entry requirements for travel to the United States were drastically tightened. The new visa regulations also affect foreign students and researchers who want to study or work in the United States. It takes much longer for visa applications to be approved, delaying and sometimes preventing the start of research activities in the United States. This national security measure has severely reduced the number of foreign researchers in the United States, though the drop does not reflect a waning interest in the United States as a research site. The United States has since made a greater effort to facilitate entry for top researchers without entailing a security risk.

The EU and the United States have cooperated in the area of graduate studies since 1996, but the projects initiated since 2001 have reached a new level of quality. The only way to preserve crucial training programs and maintain competitiveness is to guarantee the international exchange of knowledge—which pays dividends for both sides.[141] Despite the difficulties posed by empty coffers and the new U.S. entry requirements, among other things, the array of options offered by project partners on both sides of the Atlantic has done much to enhance cooperation in higher education. At the same time, however, competition for the brightest minds and for research funds is also intensifying.

Tourism

Tourism constitutes a growth factor worldwide, despite occasional slumps in the wake of the September 11 attacks and high energy costs. The United States still outranks other nations in revenues from tourism ($65 billion in 2003), followed by Spain ($42 billion), France ($37 billion), Italy ($31 billion) and Germany ($23 billion). France was the most popular travel destination, with 75 million foreign visi-

---

140 European Commission 2003.
141 European Commission: Education and Training: Programs and Actions: Other idustrialised countries: Cooperation with industrialised countries, www.europa. eu.int/comm/education/programmes/eu°thers/index_en.html (accessed January 13, 2005).

tor arrivals[142] in 2003, followed by Spain (52 million) and the United States (41 million).[143]

As for transatlantic tourism patterns, the European statistics agency Eurostat has recorded a drop in the number of U.S. tourists traveling to Europe. Only in Germany (12 percent of all tourists) and Great Britain (24 percent) does the United States top the list of visiting nationalities. Approximately 15 percent fewer U.S. tourists traveled to France, Italy, Germany and Spain in 2002 than in 2001.

Although fear of terrorist attacks may have been one reason for many U.S. travelers to avoid intercontinental flights, such concerns cannot be considered the only reason for this drop in the number of visitors: In the same period, the number of U.S. residents traveling to Japan rose by 21 percent (it dropped back to its previous level in 2004). The number traveling to the Bahamas rose by 43 percent (and by 82 percent from 2001 to 2004). South Korea saw a 15 percent increase (and eight percent in 2004) and Singapore a 14 percent increase (though the number in 2004 was 16 percent below the 2001 level).[144] Though many U.S. vacationers still choose Europe, the EU states have become less important as tourist destinations.[145]

In the opposite direction, in 2002 some 7.1 EU citizens visited the United States as tourists. If the acceding countries are included, the number rises to a good 7.4 million.[146]

In 2004, Western Europe sent the greatest number of travelers to the United States from abroad—around 9.3 million travelers, or approximately 46 percent of the total. Asia ranked second, with 5.8 million inbound travelers.[147] The most important European countries of origin were Great Britain with 4.3 million, Germany with 1.3 mil-

---

142 All arrivals from abroad, regardless of reason for travel (business, tourism, etc.)
143 World Tourism Organization 2004, 4.
144 U.S. Department of Commerce, Office of Travel and Tourism Industries: Select Destinations Visited by U.S. Resident Travelers 2001–2002, 2004, http://tinet.ita. doc.gov/view/f-2003-07-001/index.html (accessed January 13, 2005); http://tinet. ita. doc.gov/view/f-2004-11-001/index.html (accessed September 12, 2005).
145 Schmidt 2004, 3.
146 U.S. Citizen and Immigration Services: U.S. Citizenship and Immigration: Fiscal Year 2002 Yearbook of Immigration: Nonimmigrants: Table 25, http://uscis.gov/ graphics/shared/aboutus/statistics/TEMP02yrbk/TEMPExcel/Table 25.xls (accessed January 13, 2005).
147 U.S. Department of Commerce, Office of Travel and Tourism Industries: 2004 Profile of Overseas Travelers to the U.S.-Inbound, http://tinet.ita.doc.gov/view/ f-2004-07-001/index.html (accessed January 13, 2005).

lion and France with 775,000 inbound travelers to the United States. But during 2003 the number of overseas arrivals in the United States dropped steeply—by as much as 20 percent or more at the start of the Iraq war. Not until October 2003 did the number of inbound travelers return to the previous year's level. However, the total number of inbound travelers to the United States from every world region except Western Europe dropped in 2003.[148]

The planned large-scale withdrawal of U.S. troops from Western Europe will further reduce the number of U.S. residents vacationing in Europe. Tens of thousands of GIs have been stationed in Germany alone—a factor whose influence not only on travel plans but also on the emotional connection between the United States and Europe must not be underestimated.

Successes in cultural cooperation

The cultural ties between the old and the new world still have strong roots in many areas of society. Despite the tense political climate, the number of sister-city partnerships between Europe and the United States continues to climb. Such partnerships build on enduring good relationships and give them an additional stable foundation. But at the same time, they represent just one stone in the mosaic of cultural and social links spanning the two continents. They may temporarily stem the creeping erosion of transatlantic relations, but in the long run they can neither prevent it nor halt it. Likewise, the cooperation between the EU and the United States in the area of higher education and research is but a superficial indicator of mutually fruitful relations. The large number of graduate students and researchers crossing the Atlantic in both directions for research and work is less the reflection of a win-win situation than testimony to growing competition between their systems of higher education and the associated research opportunities in Europe and the United States. So far, the United States has an unmistakable lead, as the steady influx of highly qualified young researchers confirms.

---

148 U.S. Department of Commerce, Office of Travel and Tourism Industries: International Arrivals to the United States—Fourth Quarter and Annual 2003, http://tinet.ita.doc.gov/view/f-2003-400/index.html (accessed January 13, 2005).

It is no easy matter to pin down shifting patterns in transatlantic cultural cooperation, for cultural relations are a long-term phenomenon best measured by long-term indicators. However, the very resilience of cultural cooperation to day-to-day political events and crises makes it all the more useful as an indicator for the overall course of transatlantic relations. Most often, if cultural and social cooperation shows signs of disrepair, bilateral relations have suffered lasting damage that in turn has direct repercussions for cooperation between governments.

Examples of transnational problem areas: Much good will, or true cooperation?

Global problems such as poverty, migration and pollution pose an ever-growing threat to humanity in the 21st century. By all expectations, given their history over the past five decades, the United States and Europe should stand as two strong partners in the battle against these global challenges. But cooperation and coordination, once the hallmarks of transatlantic relations, have given way to parallel campaigns and even to rivalries. It seems that good will is merely put on for show. A new standard for constructive collaboration is far on the horizon.

Migration as a problem area

When it comes to constructive collaboration, security policy is not the only possible frame of reference. One of many others that could take its place is the common goal of overcoming global challenges.

Migration is one of these challenges.[149] According to the U.N. Population Division, the number of international migrants—that is, people who live for more than 12 months outside their native land or country of citizenship—rose from 154 million in 1990 to 175 million in 2000 (three percent of the world's population). Of these worldwide migrants, approximately 60 percent live in the developed nations, including 56 million in Europe and 41 million in North America. The most important distinction here is between economically motivated

149 See also Süssmuth and Weidenfeld 2005.

migration and migration for other reasons (e.g., bringing families together). More than 90 percent of migrants emigrate voluntarily.[150]

There are two extreme responses to the prospect of increasing migration in the 21st century, and both are misleading. The total rejection of immigrants deprives receiving nations of the energy and dynamism that new immigrants bring. By contrast, the establishment of free and open borders stirs up anxiety among the resident population and feeds the danger of violence, as happened in the past in the traditional immigration countries after mass immigrations.

Most countries are involved in the migration process in one of three ways: as the destination of migrants, as their country of origin or as a transit land. To coordinate the transnational flow of people in a way that benefits all sides, ongoing bilateral, regional and global discussions are necessary. An important component of this sustainable management of migration—which until now has merely meant adjusting the laws that govern it—is the joint calculation of its costs and benefits.

Since September 11, 2001, a new fear of foreigners has emerged: the fear that they might be potential terrorists. As a result of the terrorist attacks, governments in North America and Europe have acquired new powers to identify potential terrorists within their borders or keep them from crossing the borders. But closing borders for fear of terrorists is not an option, and governments on both sides of the Atlantic are trying to strike a balance between openness to foreigners and protection of their own populations.

The United States and Europe will remain important destinations for migrants. This could induce them to tackle the management of migration in a transatlantic dialogue and in cooperation. In any case, the migration policies of both partners must anticipate the prospect of continued migration in the future.

Thus, they should set clear priorities for the admission of foreigners. The goal should be to facilitate the admission of those they want and at the same time to deter others, particularly those that could represent a security risk. Such a balance of deterrence and facilitated admission might be more effective if the transatlantic partners established permanent bilateral forums for cooperation on migration issues, complemented by regional and global forums as well.

150 Martin 2004, 321–339.

A second area for transatlantic cooperation and exchange is the integration of immigrants. Integration means change: The migrants, with their diverse national, ethnic and religious backgrounds, must adjust to life in their receiving country; the admitting countries must go through an equally difficult adjustment to adapt to the presence of immigrants. The exchange of best practices for the integration of migrants would be very helpful here.

Also essential is transatlantic cooperation to prevent the drain of human resources from developing nations to industrialized countries. If the better educated simply leave, with no compensation to the developing country for the loss of that vital human capital, global inequality and the pressure to migrate will further increase. Therefore, it is crucial to develop strategies for cooperating with the sending nations to ensure that the emigrants return (bringing technology and know-how with them).

Environmental protection as a problem area

The environment also ranks high on the global agenda. Although the transatlantic partners recognize the need for constructive strategies to resolve the global environmental problems of the 21st century, they have managed to implement concrete solutions only peripherally. Few issues in recent years have caused as much contention in the transatlantic relationship. Disputes over environmental issues ranging from climate change, biodiversity and genetic engineering to the precautionary principle and the argued need for a multilateral environmental organization to complement the World Trade Organization have brought a distinct chill to transatlantic cooperation.[151]

One major source of tension is the Bush administration's withdrawal from the Kyoto Protocol. Aside from this decision, which drew a storm of media attention, the EU and the United States disagree on a number of other environmental issues.[152] These include the EU ban on importing hormone-fed beef from the United States, the regulations governing biotechnology in general and genetically modified

---

151 Steinberg 2003, 27; www.cap.lmu.de/download/2003/2003_Miami_Steinberg.pdf (accessed January 13, 2005).
152 Esty 2004, 309–321.

food in particular, the new labeling requirement for such food in the EU, the proper use of the precautionary principle and whether and how to create a Global Environmental Organization.[153]

The different views on environmental protection held in the EU and the United States and the resulting divergence in their strategic approach to problems stand out starkly in the example of the precautionary principle. According to the EU Treaty, environmental policy within the European Union is based on that principle, which justifies early action to prevent harm and an unacceptable impact to the environment or human health in the face of scientific uncertainty.[154]

Applying this principle, the European Union can proceed differently and more rapidly than the United States in setting environmental policy. The cornerstones of European environmental policy are thus quite broad, covering almost all known environmental problems. These include tackling climate protection and global warming, protecting the natural habitat and wildlife, addressing environmental and health issues, preserving natural resources and managing waste.[155]

The support of the economic community for environmental protection is of crucial importance. Starting from the assumption that, in principle, businesses have environmental awareness, the European Union seeks to sharpen and promote that awareness. Even though in general it relies on voluntary commitment on the part of businesses, the EU nevertheless endorses implementation of Europe-wide standards that allow tough action based on the principle "the polluter pays." Businesses should and must shoulder part of the responsibility for environmental policy. The European Union apparently recognizes its global responsibility as one of the world's leading economic powers and has the will to discharge that responsibility.

It would probably be unfair to say that the United States lacks that will. Nevertheless, the environmental approach of the Bush administration reveals a different set of priorities. It is particularly evident that the United States does not espouse the precautionary principle. On the contrary: It sets much greater store by scientific facts. In its

153 Ibid.
154 European Commission: Choices for a Greener Future: The European Union and the Environment. From the series Europe on the Move, 2002, www.europa.eu.int/comm/publications/booklets/move/32/txt_en.pdf (accessed January 13, 2005).
155 European Union: Activities: Environment: Our Future, Our Choice 05/04, www.europa.eu.int/pol/env/overview_en.htm (accessed January 31, 2005).

view, effective environmental strategies can be developed only after the connection between human behavior and environmental damage is proven beyond doubt. Such thinking is one reason that the United States decided to withdraw from the Kyoto Protocol.

Proceeding from this stance, Washington has laid out an environmental agenda not fundamentally different from that of the EU. The Bush administration's program includes proposals for improved air quality, water quality and ocean conservation, along with "a realistic, growth-oriented approach to global climate change."[156] But its rejection of the precautionary principle means that it does not implement preventive measures to protect the environment. Instead, it gives greater weight to environmental research and development.

However, despite their divergent approaches to tackling environmental problems and their different attitudes toward the Kyoto Protocol, the EU and the United States can look back on a long history of successful cooperation in this area. The 1974 Exchange of Letters on the Environment between the European Commission and the U.S. government established a framework for transatlantic cooperation on environmental matters. The adoption of the New Transatlantic Agenda and its Joint Action Plan in 1995 opened up further possibilities for coordination and cooperation on environmental issues.

Although the U.S. decision to back away from the Kyoto Protocol stopped transatlantic cooperation in its tracks, the two partners emphasized at a subsequent summit meeting that the problem of global climate change would remain on the agenda and that the search for appropriate strategies must continue. One outcome of the summit was an agreement to establish a mechanism for dialogue. The first meeting of the EU–US High-Level Representatives on Climate Change convened in April 2002.[157]

Nevertheless, the prevailing antagonism between the United States and the EU puts environmental protection at risk. Clearly, environmental problems spill over local and national boundaries and cannot be solved on a national level. Many of the most pressing environmental problems have international repercussions that make

---

156 The White House: Protecting our Nation's Environment, www.whitehouse. gov/ infocus/environment/index-cont.html (accessed January 13, 2005).

157 European Commission: Environment: Policies: International Issues: International Relations: Bilateral Relations—USA 08/07/03, www.europa.eu.int/comm/environ ment/international_issues/relations_usa_en.htm (accessed January 13, 2005).

international cooperation an absolute necessity. Specifically in this regard, an EU–U.S. initiative could create a stronger system of international environmental governance that could identify the most important environmental problems and promote cooperation in those areas.[158]

Another crucial reason for transatlantic cooperation lies in the impact of a nation's environmental policy on trade relations. Unless regulations and standards are carefully thought through, they can quickly become trade barriers. International environmental cooperation thus constitutes an important counterpart to international economic cooperation.

Given the necessity of cooperation between the United States and the EU in this area, the lack of an overarching commitment to solving global environmental problems and the absence of a corresponding joint strategy is casting a pall over transatlantic relations. Precisely here, a transatlantic learning community in which experiences, data and information can be exchanged and compared can only pay dividends.[159]

The question of the "why" behind decisions is a valid one—and not only in the area of environmental policy. It applies to a host of global issues that raise transatlantic problems. Although the examples of migration and environmental protection explored here are but a small sampling, they nonetheless give a good picture of the current character of transatlantic relations.

While the European Union has increasingly come into its own, and by no means lags behind the United States in its strategies for solving sociopolitical problems, the United States nowadays appears to give lower priority to solving global problems—except for international terrorism. Although the imperative need for transatlantic cooperation is as obvious as its long-term dividends for both the United States and the EU, cooperation between the two partners still occurs only in those areas where a clear, economically quantifiable benefit can be identified. Actual constructive cooperation, however, is sadly wanting.

---

158 Transatlantic Strategy Group on Security and on Economics, Finance and Trade 2003.
159 Esty 2004, 311.

Outlook: into the future with pragmatism and strategic realism

Do the transatlantic partners still belong together in the 21st century? And what role will Europe play in the transatlantic relationship? Naturally, the United States would find it useful to have a European partner that could share the burden of problem solving. The United States continues to seek a division of labor when it comes to Iraq, conflict-ridden Africa and the nuclear arms ambitions of North Korea and Iran. Washington wants functional partnerships in the fight against terrorism and on such issues as AIDS, the drug trade and migration. But is Europe capable of such a problem-solving partnership? The very question reveals the Europeans' deficit: not the lack of international potential, but the lack of strategic orientation. The Europeans do not think in the categories of world politics. Equally lacking is a sober, clear definition of their interests.

Thus, the Europeans introduced a common currency—without debating economic and monetary policy. (Hence the composure with which the United States hears speculation about the euro as a global currency reserve.) Thus, the Europeans established their own military force for crisis intervention—but scrimped on equipment and infrastructure. Thus, a constitutional assembly convened representatives from all across Europe for more than a year to hammer out a draft for a European constitution. But in the home stretch of ratification, European citizens nixed the proposed text—whereupon the whole project was put on ice.

A strategic elite that could establish conceptual foundations is nowhere in sight. Thus, each side needs the other to compensate for its own deficits. If the Europeans and the Americans can recognize this with equal clarity, they can seize this situation as the opportunity to overcome their deficits and make a fresh start.

One possible outcome is still a structural asymmetry. The world power—the United States—would welcome an easing of the strategic burden, which, however, Europe cannot provide. But in contrast to previous decades, the two partners no longer need each other to maintain the internal political stability that inevitably existed under the political and military East-West constellation of that era. The logical consequence is a moderate and limited connection between the two partners. The reality of events has left the old sentimental attachment far behind. Europe, too, has bid farewell to this old sentiment and faced up to the new reality.

At the very latest, this became clear with the terrorist attacks of September 11, 2001. On that day, transatlantic relations acquired a new overarching bond in the form of a common threat, and international terrorism took center stage as the dominant security problem of the Western world. However, this new common security threat did not have the effect of revitalizing a shared security policy in the transatlantic alliance. On the contrary: The different perceptions of the threat and risks that terrorism posed, and the different security policies developed in response, have brought a new dimension to the divergence between the transatlantic partners. This has not necessarily led to a new American isolationism or an anti-European stance. Europe simply has been booted from its earlier privileged position into a more normal reality based on national interests. If the situation allows, Washington now prefers to seek cooperation in an à la carte multilateralism.

In view of the recent political ill feelings between the transatlantic partners over the Iraq war, but also in light of conflicts over trade, the question arises whether the transatlantic relationship is on the brink of a permanent split. Will the political and economic quarrels actually lead these two key political partners to part ways?

Security policy considerations

From the security policy perspective, the answer is no. America needs Europe's help. In launching the Iraq war, even the sole world power took on too much. The costs placed an alarming burden on the national budget. According to recent reports, the war in Iraq is consuming approximately $5.6 billion dollars every month. For that reason alone, a new version of the decades-old practice of burden sharing inevitably comes to mind. Furthermore, the appalling images of the victims of terrorism in Iraq torment American sensitivities. President George W. Bush will not have much more time to turn the corner in Iraq—otherwise, the American public will veer sharply against him and view the war as a mistake of historic proportions.

This is particularly true because the original justification for the war on Iraq—that Saddam Hussein was in possession of weapons of mass destruction—could not be substantiated later. Even now, President Bush has had to acknowledge that the majority of Americans no longer unconditionally support his course in the war on terrorism. Public opinion tipped against him in August 2005, when polls found that not even 40 percent of the population still supported the Iraq war. George W. Bush is under immense pressure. Open criticism of his handling of the war against terrorism has steadily mounted in recent months—even among the ranks of Republicans.

The criticism intensified yet again in August 2005, when Hurricane Katrina struck the southern United States, devastating an area the size of Great Britain. The whole world looked on as tens of thousands of U.S. citizens were stranded without food, water and aid in flooded New Orleans. The images streaming across the media called to mind disaster areas in the third world. The world's mightiest nation floundered for days before it managed to coordinate the first rescue measures. Who could fail to hear the accusations that National Guard troops—now urgently needed by their fellow citizens—had instead been deployed thousands of miles away to rebuild a foreign country?

With a reversal of public opinion looming in the United States, President Bush cannot afford to have his initiatives in the Near East perceived as the Americans largely going it alone. He must frame the undertaking in the larger perspective of the entire free world. For that, he needs Europe. To satisfy the exigencies of domestic politics in the United States, he must convince its European partner to participate in the reconstruction of Iraq. The American public is demanding that its president find partners to help shoulder the burden of Iraq.

Thus, the charm offensive that George W. Bush staged during his visit to Europe in February 2005 had a core of purely political interests. Simmering beneath the surface of this cordiality, however, are a multitude of global political conflicts that urgently require a transatlantic rapprochement: Iran's potential production of nuclear weapons, the arms embargo against China, the transformation of the Near and Middle East, reform of the United Nations, international climate protection.

Never before has the global political agenda included so many issues at once. Until now, however, Europe and the United States have held no substantive strategic dialogue about any of these challenges. In the future, there must be a locus of strategic understanding across the Atlantic—a place that offers opportunities for informal and confidential exchange. In that forum, it must be possible to identify problems freely and openly, away from media publicity, and in the best case, to deal with them before they put a strain on the relationship. The fact that such a forum does not yet exist is the central deficit of the transatlantic partnership.

But despite all the asymmetries described here, this much can be said: America needs Europe, and not just for the reconstruction of Iraq—other areas are also crucial. Europe has begun to learn how to act in the arena of world politics. Testimony to this is provided by the negotiations that Europe—represented by France, Great Britain and Germany, along with Javier Solana, the EU's high representative for the common foreign and security policy—held with Iran regarding compliance with the International Atomic Energy Agency (IAEA) resolution that prohibited Iran's resumption of uranium conversion activities for military purposes. The United States, having broken off diplomatic relations with Iran, could not participate in official negotiations and was compelled to rely on the negotiating skills of the Europeans. Washington repeatedly emphasized that it expressly supported the process and the course taken by its European partner.

From this precedent, it may be possible to derive the initial contours of future strategic cooperation between the Americans and the Europeans: Both sides take responsibility for resolving global conflicts. They divide responsibility among themselves for negotiating with the conflicting parties in the various regions of crisis. They work together to reach agreement on procedures, options and goals. The United States benefits because it need not shoulder the burden of global crisis management alone; the Europeans, for their part, gain clout on the stage of world politics. At the same time, they benefit from a strong negotiating position: If the other party to the negotiations rejects a political solution, the threat of military action by the United States waits in the wings.

From the economic perspective as well, a break in transatlantic relationships appears unlikely. The reason is simple: Neither side can afford to let political resentment damage a long tradition of good trade relations and strong economic ties. Independent of any arguments over military and economic strength, one essential element of the transatlantic connection remains unmistakable: A healthy relationship is vital to the economic interests of both sides.

Even at a time when political decision-makers have been colliding with their counterparts on the other side of the ocean, each side's economic interest in the other's prosperity reached a high point in the last 10 years—despite the fact that the connecting cement of a common Soviet threat has crumbled away.

The economic data speak for themselves: The European market supplies more than 50 percent of American companies' revenues. Europe remains the most important partner for American businesses. European companies provide more than a million jobs in California alone. European investments in Texas exceed the entire U.S. investments in Japan. On both sides of the Atlantic, more than 12.5 million people make their living on transatlantic economic connections.[160]

Thus, even its own national interests impel the United States to support the deepening and widening of the European Union. The United States also will profit when advances in European integration make it impossible for the slowest ship in the European fleet to block future-oriented strategies of transatlantic economic cooperation.

The EU's enlargement is also in the vital interest of the United States. The absorption of new members from Eastern Europe will greatly increase their inner stability and significantly reduce the possibility of crises and conflicts in the region. The United States has a particular stake in the latter because—as the Balkan wars demonstrated—the resolution of crises of such proportions in Europe most probably still requires the direct engagement of the United States. At every future opportunity, therefore, the United States will continue to urge the EU to hasten its accession of Eastern European nations.

The day-to-day political actionism and the resulting media headlines can be deceptive, since they hide the fact that an intact relation-

160 See Patten and Lamy 2003; Scherpenberg 2000.

ship remains behind the torn façade. Reciprocal international invest-ments—not trade in specific goods—are the backbone of the transat-lantic economic partnership. Even the rising Asian market cannot upset this solid foundation. Unless or until the European market shrinks, American economic activities will remain focused to a con-siderable degree on Europe.

The turbulence of recent years has set these two partners at odds. Out of this rivalry, however, a new cooperation can grow. The 21st century, with all its foreign and domestic challenges, offers Euro-peans and Americans alike every opportunity for this renewal. The first indications have already come into view. The waves of agitation have subsided; the tone has moderated. The seismographs show that the United States and Europe are moving toward each other again. Both sides know that they need each other. Both know that no com-petitive alternative to transatlantic cooperation exists.

If this cooperation—not only between the United States and Ger-many, but also with the European Union—is to stabilize again and attain a new dynamic, it must begin with the espousal of a steadfast pragmatism and strategic realism. The Europeans, in particular, must first internalize this rational approach. If the endeavor suc-ceeds, the start of the 21st century can ring in a new—and success-ful—era in the history of transatlantic relations.

Bibliography

Adams, Willi Paul. Die USA im 21. Jahrhundert. In *Grundriss der Geschichte*. Vol. 29. Munich, 2000.

Adams, Willi Paul, and Peter Lösche (eds.). *Länderbericht USA. Geschichte – Politik. Geographie – Wirtschaft. Gesellschaft – Kultur.* 3rd ed. Frankfurt am Main and New York, 1999.

Ahearn, Raymond. US–European Union Trade Relations: Issues and Policy Challenges. *Issue Brief for Congress* 2003: 6.

Alfred Herrhausen Gesellschaft (eds.). *Europa – Global Player oder Statist der Weltpolitik?* Frankfurt am Main, 2003.

Algieri, Franco. Die Reform der GASP – Anleitung zu begrenztem gemeinsamen Handeln. In *Amsterdam in der Analyse,* edited by Werner Weidenfeld. Gütersloh, 1998: 89–120.

Algieri, Franco. Die Europäische Sicherheits- und Verteidigungspolitik – erweiterter Handlungsspielraum für die GASP. In *Nizza in der Analyse,* edited by Werner Weidenfeld. Gütersloh, 2001: 161–202.

Andrews, David M. (ed.). *The Atlantic Alliance Under Stress: Relations after Iraq.* New York, 2005.

Asmus, Ronald D. *Rethinking the EU: Why Washington Needs to Support European Integration.* Oxford, 2005.

Barber, Benjamin R. *Imperium der Angst. Die USA und die Neuordnung der Welt.* Munich, 2003.

Behr, Timo. U.S. Attitudes Towards Europe: A Shift of Paradigms? *Research and European Issues,* No. 29. 2003: 70.

Bender, Peter. *Weltmacht Amerika. Das Neue Rom.* Stuttgart, 2003.

Berg, Manfred. Die innere Entwicklung. Vom Zweiten Weltkrieg bis zur Watergate-Krise 1974. In *Länderbericht USA. Geschichte – Politik. Geographie – Wirtschaft. Gesellschaft – Kultur,* edited by Willi Paul Adams and Peter Lösche. 3rd ed. Frankfurt am Main and New York, 1999: 144–168.

Bertelsmann Europa-Kommission (eds.). *Europas Vollendung vorberei-ten. Anforderungen an die Regierungskonferenz 2000.* Gütersloh, 2000.

Bertelsmann Foundation (eds.). *Enhancing the European Union as an International Security Actor. A Strategy for Action.* Gütersloh, 2000.

Bertelsmann Foundation, Bertelsmann Group for Policy Research and German Marshall Fund of the United States (eds.): Migration in the New Millennium. Recommendations of the Transatlantic Learning Community. Gütersloh, 2000.

Bertelsmann Stiftung (eds.). *Bertelsmann Transformation Index 2006: Auf dem Weg zur marktwirtschaftlichen Demokratie.* Gütersloh, 2005.

Blix, Hans. *Mission Irak. Wahrheit und Lügen.* Munich, 2004.

Bohrer, Karl Heinz, and Kurt Scheel (eds.). Europa oder Amerika? Zur Zukunft des Westens. *Merkur, Deutsche Zeitschrift für Europäisches Denken.* (54) Special Issue 9/10: 299, 2000.

Brzezinski, Zbigniew. *The Choice: Global Domination or Global Leadership.* New York, 2004.

Buchheit, Eva. *Der Briand-Kellogg-Pakt von 1928 – Machtpolitik oder Friedensstreben?* Münster, 1998.

Bücherl, Wolfgang. Eine Allianz für Amerika? Die NATO nach Prag. *Internationale Politik* (58) 3: 55–59, 2003.

Bush, George W. *The George W. Bush Foreign Policy Reader: Presidential Speeches and Commentary,* edited by John W. Dietrich. Armonk, N.Y., 2005.

Calleo, David P. *Rethinking Europe's Future.* Princeton, 2001.

Cameron, Fraser. *US Foreign Policy after the Cold War. Global Hegemon or Reluctant Sheriff?* London and New York, 2002.

Carey, David, and Harry Tchilinguirian. Average Effective Tax Rates on Capital, Labour and Consumption. *Economic Department Working Papers* No. 258, Oct. 10, 2000.

Curti, Merle. *The Growth of American Thought.* New Brunswick, 1991.

Czempiel, Ernst-Otto. *Kluge Macht. Außenpolitik für das 21. Jahrhundert.* Munich, 1999.

Daalder, Ivo H. The End of Atlanticism. *Survival* (2) 147–166, 2003a.

Daalder, Ivo H., and James M. Lindsay. *America Unbound. The Bush Revolution in Foreign Policy.* Brookings Institution. Washington, D.C., 2003b.

Dassù, Marta, and Roberto Menotti. Europe and America in the age of Bush. *Survival* (47) 1: 105–122, 2005.

Dembinski, Matthias, Peter Rudolf and Jürgen Wilzewski (eds.). *Amerikanische Weltpolitik nach dem Ost-West-Konflikt*. Baden-Baden, 1994.

Dembinski, Matthias, and Wolfgang Wagner. Europäische Kollateralschäden. Zur Zukunft der europäischen Außen-, Sicherheits- und Verteidigungspolitik nach dem Irak-Krieg. *Aus Politik und Zeitgeschichte* (B 31–32): 31–38, 2003.

Dittgen, Herbert. *Amerikanische Demokratie und Weltpolitik. Außenpolitik der Vereinigten Staaten*. Paderborn, 1998.

Esty, Daniel C. Bridging the transatlantic environmental divide. In *From Alliance to Coalitions – The Future of Transatlantic Relations*, edited by Werner Weidenfeld, Caio Koch-Weser, C. Fred Bergsten, Walther Stützle and John Hamre. Gütersloh, 2004: 309–321.

Euractive, "Accession talks proper all set to start for Croatia and Turkey," 8 February, 2006, www.euractive.com (accessed February 14, 2006).

Euractive, "WTO ruling on tax subsidies sparks EU/US trade flareup", 14.02.06, www.euractive.com (accessed February 15, 2006).

Europäische Kommission. Keine Forschung ohne Forscher. *FTE. info, Magazin über europäische Forschung. Humanressourcen*. Special Issue, August 2003: 23.

Europäische Kommission. Städtepartnerschaften: Anzahl der von 2001 bis 2003 eingereichten Anträge für Städtepartnerschaftsprojekte 08/04. www.europa.eu.int/comm/dgs/education_culture/towntwin/ doc/projects01_en.pdf (accessed January 13, 2005).

Europäische Kommission. *Weichenstellungen für eine umweltgerechte Zukunft. Die Europäische Union und die Umwelt*. Brussels, 2002. Also online under: www.europa.eu.int/comm/publications/book lets/move/32/txt_de.pdf (accessed January 13, 2005).

Europäische Union. Tätigkeitsbereich Umwelt: Unsere Zukunft liegt in unserer Hand 05/04. www.europa.eu.int/pol/env/overview_de. htm (accessed January 13, 2005).

European Commission: Education and Training: Programmes and Actions: EU–USA: The EU–US Cooperation Programme in Higher Education and Vocational Education Training 2001–2005. www. europa.eu.int/comm/education/programmes/eu-usa/index_en. html (accessed January 13, 2005).

European Commission. Environment: Policies: International Issues: International Relations: Bilateral Relations – USA 08/07/03. www.

europa.eu.int/comm/environment/international_issues/relations_usa_en.htm (accessed January 13, 2005).

European Commission. European Union Factsheet: EU–US Bilateral Economic Relations. http://trade-info.cec.eu.int/doclib/docs/2003/october/tradoc_114064.pdf (accessed January 13, 2005).

European Commission. European Union: Factsheet: US Non-Compliance with WTO Rulings. http://trade-info.cec.eu.int/doclib/docs/2003/october/tradoc_114065.pdf (accessed January 13, 2005).

European Commission. External Trade: WTO Dispute Settlement, What's New? September 13, 2002. www.europa.eu.int/comm/trade/miti/dis pute/pr130902_de.htm (accessed January 13, 2005).

European Commission. *Key Figures 2003–2004. Towards a European Research Area. Science, Technology and Innovation.* Brussels, 2003.

European Commission. Sectoral Issues: Trade in agricultural goods and fishery products. August 13, 2003. www.europa.eu.int/comm/trade/issues/sectoral/agri_fish/pr140803_en.htm (accessed January 13, 2005).

European Commission. The EU's relations with the United States of America. Joint EU–US Action Plan, IV. Building Bridges Across the Atlantic. www.europa.eu.int/comm/external_relations/us/action_plan/4_building_bridges.htm (accessed January 13, 2005).

European Commission. Trade Issues: Bilateral Trade Relations: USA. www.europa.eu.int/comm/trade/issues/bilateral/countries/usa/index_en.htm (accessed January 13, 2005).

European Commission. Trade Issues: Respecting the Rules: WTO Dispute Settlement. February 27, 2004. www.europa.eu.int/comm/trade/issues/respectrules/dispute/pr270204_en.htm (accessed January 13, 2005).

European Economic Group CESifo. *Report on the European Economy 2004.* Munich, 2004.

Ferguson, Niall. *Das verleugnete Imperium. Chancen und Risiken amerikanischer Macht.* Berlin, 2004.

Forndran, Erhard. Kontinuitäten und Veränderungen in den transatlantischen Beziehungen seit 1918. In *Transatlantische Beziehungen,* edited by Manfred Knapp. Stuttgart, 1990: 9–36.

Fukuyama, Francis. *Staaten bauen. Die neue Herausforderung internationaler Beziehungen.* Berlin, 2004.

Garton Ash, Timothy. *Freie Welt. Europa, Amerika und die Chance der Krise.* Munich, 2004.

Giering, Claus (ed.). *Der EU-Reformkonvent – Analyse und Dokumentation*. CD-ROM. Gütersloh, 2003.

Giering, Claus. Die institutionellen Reformen von Nizza – Anforderungen, Ergebnisse, Konsequenzen. In *Nizza in der Analyse*, edited by Werner Weidenfeld. Gütersloh, 2001: 51–144.

Giering, Claus. *Europa zwischen Zweckverband und Superstaat. Die Entwicklung der politikwissenschaftlichen Integrationstheorie im Prozeß der europäischen Integration*. Bonn, 1997.

Göler, Daniel, and Mathias Jopp. Der Konvent und die Europäische Verfassung. In *Jahrbuch der Europäischen Integration 2002/2003*, edited by Werner Weidenfeld and Wolfgang Wessels. Bonn, 2003: 35–46.

Gordon, Bernard K. A High-Risk Trade Policy. *Foreign Affairs* (4) 105–118, 2003.

Gordon, Philip H., and Jeremy Shapiro. *Allies at War: America, Europe, and the Crisis over Iraq*. New York, 2004.

Habermas, Jürgen. *Der gespaltene Westen. Kleine Politische Schriften X*. Frankfurt am Main, 2004.

Hacke, Christian. *Zur Weltmacht verdammt. Die amerikanische Außenpolitik von J. F. Kennedy bis G. W. Bush*. Berlin, 2005.

Hallstein, Walter. *Der unvollendete Bundesstaat. Europäische Erfahrungen und Erkenntnisse*. Munich, 1994.

Hamilton, Daniel S., and Joseph P. Quinlan. *Partners in Prosperity. The Changing Geography of the Transatlantic Economy*. Center for Transatlantic Relations, Johns Hopkins University, Paul H. Nitze School of Advanced International Studies, 2004.

Hanrieder, Wolfram F. *Deutschland. Europa. Amerika. Die Außenpolitik der Bundesrepublik Deutschland 1949–1994*. 2nd ed. Paderborn, Munich, Vienna, Zurich, 1995.

Heisbourg, François. European defence: making it work. *Chaillot Papers* No. 42, September 2000.

Heisbourg, François. US-European relations: from lapsed alliance to new partnership? *International Politics* (41) 1: 119–126, 2004.

Herzinger, Richard. Siamesische Zwillinge. Europa und Amerika streiten sich heftig – und gehören doch zusammen. *Internationale Politik* (58) 6: 1–8, 2003.

Holz, Kurt A. *Die Diskussion um den Dawes- und Young-Plan in der deutschen Presse*. Frankfurt am Main, 1977.

Hongju Koh, Harold. Die Bewahrung amerikanischer Werte. Herausforderungen im Innern und Äußern. Das Zeitalter des Terrors. in

Amerika und die Welt nach dem 11. September, edited by Strobe Tal-bott and Nayan Chanda. Munich and Berlin, 2002: 138–161.

Howorth, Jolyon. European integration and defence: the ultimate challenge? *Chaillot Papers* No. 43, November 2000.

Hunter, Robert E. The US and the European Union: Bridging the strategic gap. *The International Spectator* (1) 35–50, 2004.

Huntington, Samuel. *Who Are We? Die Krise der amerikanischen Identität.* Hamburg, 2004.

International Bertelsmann Forum. Central and Eastern Europe on the Way into the European Union. Warsaw, June 25–26, 1999. Güters-loh, 1999.

Junker, Detlef. Weltwirtschaftskrise, New Deal, Zweiter Weltkrieg, 1929–1945. In *Länderbericht USA,* edited by Willi Paul Adams and Peter Lösche. Frankfurt am Main and New York, 1999: 164–185.

Junker, Detlef. *Power and Mission. Was Amerika antreibt.* Freiburg im Breisgau, 2003.

Kagan, Robert. *Of Paradise and Power. America and Europe in the New World Order.* New York, 2003.

Kamp, Karl-Heinz. Von der Prävention zur Präemption? Die neue amerikanische Sicherheitsstrategie. *Internationale Politik* (57) 12: 19–24, 2002.

Kaplan, Lawrence S. *NATO Divided, NATO United: the Evolution of an Alliance.* Westport, Conn., 2004.

Kennedy, Paul M. *Aufstieg und Fall der großen Mächte.* Frankfurt am Main, 2000.

Kempe, Iris. *Direkte Nachbarschaft. Die Beziehungen zwischen der Erweiterten EU und der Russischen Föderation, Ukraine, Weißrussland und Moldova.* Gütersloh, 2000.

Kempe, Iris (ed.). *Beyond EU Enlargement. Volume I: The Agenda of Direct Neighbourhood for Eastern Europe.* Gütersloh, 2001.

Kempe, Iris. *Prospects and Risks Beyond EU Enlargement. Eastern Europe: Challenges of a Pan-European Policy.* Opladen, 2003.

Kempin, Ronja, and Anja Wagner. Die transatlantischen Beziehungen nach der Irak-Krise. Aus europäischen Fachzeitschriften, 1. Halbjahr 2003. *SWP-Zeitschriftenschau,* July 2003.

Kissinger, Henry A. *Does America Need a Foreign Policy? Toward a Diplomacy for the 21st Century.* New York, 2002.

Kissinger, Henry A., and Lawrence H. Summers: *Renewing the Atlantic Partnership: Report of an Independent Task Force Sponsored by the Council on Foreign Relations.* New York, 2004.

Knapp, Manfred (ed.). *Transatlantische Beziehungen.* Stuttgart, 1990.

Kneeshaw, Stephen J. *In Pursuit of Peace. The American Reaction to the Briand-Kellogg Pact. 1928–1929.* New York, 1991.

Krell, Gert. Arroganz der Macht, Arroganz der Ohnmacht. Die Weltordnungspolitik der USA und die transatlantischen Beziehungen. *Aus Politik und Zeitgeschichte* (B 31–32) 23–30, 2003.

Kremp, Werner, and Jürgen Wilzewski (eds.). *Weltmacht vor neuer Bedrohung. Die Bush-Administration und die US-Außenpolitik nach dem Angriff auf Amerika.* Atlantische Akademie Rheinland-Pfalz, Vol. 20. Trier, 2003.

Kupchan, Charles. *Die europäische Herausforderung. Vom Ende der Vorherrschaft Amerikas.* Berlin, 2003.

Kupchan, Charles A. *The End of the American Era: U.S. Foreign Policy and the Geopolitics of the Twenty-first Century.* New York, 2002.

Kurz, Robert. *Weltordnungskrieg. Das Ende der Souveränität und die Wandlungen des Imperialismus im Zeitalter der Globalisierung.* Bad Honnef, 2003.

Larrabee, Stephen F. *NATO's Eastern Agenda in a New Strategic Era.* Santa Monica, 2003.

Larres, Klaus. USA. Die siegreiche Übermacht. *Handelsblatt,* Mar. 11–12, 2003: 8.

Lindberg, Tod (ed.). *Beyond Paradise and Power: Europe, America and the Future of a Troubled Partnership.* New York, 2004.

Lindsay, James M., and Michael E. O'Hanlon. *Defending America. The Case for Limited National Missile Defense.* Washington, D. C., 2001.

Link, Werner. *Die Neuordnung der Weltpolitik. Grundprobleme globaler Politik an der Schwelle zum 21. Jahrhundert.* Munich, 2001.

Linn, Johannes F. *Rebuilding Transatlantic Relations – It's Time to Repair Damaged Bridges.* The Brookings Institution. Washington, D. C., 2004a.

Linn, Johannes F. *Trends and Prospects of Transatlantic Economic Relations. The Glue That Cements a Fraying Partnership?* The Brookings Institution, Washington, D. C. April 28, 2004b: 2.

Lorenz, Sebastian, and Marcel Machill (eds.). *Transatlantik. Transfer von Politik, Wirtschaft und Kultur.* Opladen and Wiesbaden, 1999.

Mann, Michael. *Die ohnmächtige Supermacht. Warum die USA die Welt nicht regieren können.* Frankfurt am Main and New York, 2003.

Martens, Michael. Aus Sfor wird Eufor. *Frankfurter Allgemeine Zeitung,* Dec. 2, 2004: 5.

Martin, Philip. Immigration and Integration. In *From Alliance to Coalitions – The Future of Transatlantic Relations,* edited by Werner Weidenfeld, Caio Koch-Weser, C. Fred Bergsten, Walther Stützle and John Hamre. Gütersloh, 2004: 321–339.

Maull, Hanns W. Europe and the new balance of global order. *International Affairs* (81) 4: 775–799(25), July 2005.

Maull, Hanns W. Zivilmacht. Die Konzeption und ihre sicherheitspolitische Relevanz. In *Sicherheitspolitik Deutschlands. Neue Konstellationen, Risiken, Instrumente,* edited by Wolfgang Heydrich et al. Baden-Baden, 1992: 771–786.

Meiers, Franz-Josef. Transatlantic Relations after the US Elections: From Rift to Harmony. Discussion Paper C 140. Zentrum für Europäische Integrationsforschung, Bonn, 2004.

Meier-Walser, Reinhard C. Braucht Europa die NATO noch? *Jahrbuch für Internationale Sicherheitspolitik 2003,* edited by Erich Reiter. Vienna, 2003: 375–389.

Meier-Walser, Reinhard C. *Die Transformation der NATO. Zukunftsrelevanz, Entwicklungsperspektiven und Reformstrategien.* Hanns-Seidel-Stiftung Vol. 34. Munich, 2004.

Merkl, Peter H. *The Distracted Eagle: The Rift between America and Old Europe.* New York, 2005.

Metz, Almut, and Christina Notz. Von Nizza bis Rom. Chronologie des EU-Reformkonvents. In *Der EU-Reformkonvent – Analyse und Dokumentation,* edited by Claus Giering. CD-ROM. Gütersloh, 2003.

Meyer, Jürgen, and Sven Hölscheidt. Wie der Konvent Europa verfasst hat. *Zeitschrift für Staats- und Europawissenschaften* (1) 3: 336–346, 2003.

Meurs, Wim van. *Prospects and Risks beyond EU Enlargement. Southeastern Europe: Weak States and Strong International Support.* Opladen, 2003.

Mills, Robert J. *Health Insurance Coverage: 2001.* U.S. Census Bureau, Washington, D.C., 2002: 3.

Müller, Harald. *Amerika schlägt zurück. Die Weltordnung nach dem 11. September.* Frankfurt am Main, 2003.

Möller, Kay. Hegemoniale Herausforderung und wirtschaftliche Zusammenarbeit: Die USA und China. In *Weltmacht ohne Gegner. Amerikanische Außenpolitik zu Beginn des 21. Jahrhunderts,* edited by Peter Rudolf and Jürgen Wilzewski. Baden-Baden, 2000: 65–86.

Moravcsik, Andrew. An Ocean Apart: The United States and Europe have vital shared interests, but is the Bush administration serious about finding common ground? *The American Prospect,* March 2005.

National Commission on Terrorism. Countering the Changing Threat of International Terrorism. http://www.fas.org/irp/threat/com mission.html (accessed January 15, 2006)

Nau, Henry R. *At Home Abroad: Identity and Power in American Foreign Policy.* London and Ithaca, N.Y., 2002.

Nye, Joseph. *The Paradox of American Power: Why the World's Only Superpower Can't Go It Alone.* New York 2002.

Office of Homeland Security. National Strategy for Homeland Security. July 2002. www.whitehouse.gov/homeland/book/nat_strat_hls. pdf (accessed January 7, 2005).

Organisation for Economic Cooperation and Development (OECD). *Main Economic Indicators.* Paris, 2002.

Patten, Chris, and Pascal Lamy. Let's put away the megaphones. A trans-Atlantic appeal. *International Herald Tribune,* Apr. 9, 2003.

Pilz, Peter. *Mit Gott gegen alle. Amerikas Kampf um die Weltherrschaft.* Stuttgart and Munich, 2003.

Pond, Elizabeth. *Friendly Fire: The Near-Death of the Transatlantic Alliance.* Pittsburgh, Pa., 2004.

Powell, Colin L. Fifty years of formal United States and European Union relations and European Union accession. *DISAM Journal* (26) 4:79–82, Summer 2004.

The President of the United States. The National Security Strategy of the United States of America. September 2002. www.whitehouse. gov/nsc/nss.pdf (accessed October 1, 2002).

Proctor, Bernadette D., and Joseph Dalaker. *Poverty in the United States: 2001.* U.S. Census Bureau, Washington, D.C., 2002.

Reyn, Sebastian. *Allies or Aliens? George W. Bush and the Transatlantic Crisis in Historical Perspective.* Zoetermeer, 2004.

Rifkin, Jeremy. *Der Europäische Traum. Die Vision einer leisen Supermacht.* Frankfurt am Main, 2004.

Rimscha, Robert von. *Die Bushs. Weltmacht als Familienerbe.* Frankfurt am Main and New York, 2004.

Risse, Thomas. Es gibt keine Alternative. USA und EU müssen ihre Beziehungen neu justieren. *Internationale Politik* (58) 6: 9–18, 2003.

Ritschl, Albrecht. *Deutschlands Krise und Konjunktur. 1924–1934. Binnenkonjunktur, Auslandsverschuldung und Reparationsproblem zwischen Dawes-Plan und Transfersperre.* Berlin, 2002.

Rittberger, Volker (ed.). *Weltpolitik heute.* Baden-Baden, 2004.

Rubenfeld, J. The Two World Orders. In *Rebuilding Transatlantic Relations – It's Time to Repair Damaged Bridges,* edited by Johannes F. Linn. Washington, D.C., 2004: 3.

Rudolf, Peter, and Jürgen Wilzewski (eds.). *Weltmacht ohne Gegner. Amerikanische Außenpolitik zu Beginn des 21. Jahrhunderts.* Baden-Baden, 2000.

Rüb, Matthias. *Der atlantische Graben. Europa und Amerika auf getrennten Wegen.* Vienna, 2004.

Rühl, Lothar. *Das Reich des Guten. Machtpolitik und globale Strategie Amerikas.* Stuttgart, 2005.

Rühle, Michael. Brauchen die USA die NATO noch? In *Jahrbuch für internationale Sicherheitspolitik 2003,* edited by Erich Reiter. Vienna, 2003: 359–374.

Sale, Kirkpatrick. *The Conquest of Paradise: Christopher Columbus and the Columbian Legacy.* New York, 1990.

Samson, Ivo: Between 'Old Europe' and Transatlanticism. *WeltTrends* No. 40: 65–69, 2003.

Schauer, Hans. Europa und Amerika – Rivalen oder Partner. *Aus Politik und Zeitgeschichte* (B 29–30), 12–21: 1999.

Scherpenberg, Jens van. Konkurrenten und Partner: Die Außenwirtschaftsbeziehungen zwischen USA und EU. In *Weltmacht ohne Gegner. Amerikanische Außenpolitik zu Beginn des 21. Jahrhunderts,* edited by Peter Rudolf and Jürgen Wilzewski. Baden-Baden, 2000: 87–108.

Schley, Nicole. Die Bush-Doktrin. Amerikanische Außenpolitik unter neuen Vorzeichen. *Europäische Zeitung,* September/October 2002.

Schmid, Thomas. Ungeliebte Freundschaft. *Frankfurter Allgemeine Sonntagszeitung,* June 6, 2004.

Schmidt, Hans-Werner. Tourismus in der Europäischen Union 2003. *Eurostat: Statistik kurz gefasst. Industrie, Handel und Dienstleistungen.* Thema 4–12 2004.

Schott, Jeffrey J. *Decision Making in the WTO.* Institute for International Economics. Washington, D.C., March 2000.

Schott, Jeffrey J., and Gary Hufbauer. *Transatlantic Trade Relations: Challenges for 2003*. Institute for International Economics. Washington, D.C., 2003.

Seidelmann, Reimund. Das ESVP-Projekt und die EU-Krisenreaktionskräfte: Konstruktionsdefizite und politische Perspektiven. *integration* (25) 2: 111–124, 2002.

Singer, Peter. *Der Präsident des Guten und Bösen. Die Ethik George W. Bushs*. Erlangen, 2004.

Sloan, Stanley R. *NATO, the European Union, and the Transatlantic Community: The Transatlantic Bargain Reconsidered*. Oxford, 2003.

Solana, Javier. Die Gemeinsame Europäische Sicherheits- und Verteidigungspolitik – Das Integrationsprojekt der nächsten Dekade. *integration* (23) 1: 1–6, 2000.

Solana, Javier. Ein sicheres Europa in einer besseren Welt. European Council, Thessaloniki, June 20, 2003. http://ue.eu.int/ueDocs/cms_Data/docs/pressdata/EN/reports/76255.pdf

Speck, Ulrich, and Natan Sznaider (eds.). Empire Amerika. Perspektiven einer neuen Weltordnung. Munich, 2003.

Steinberg, James B. *The United States and Europe – an Elective Partnership*. The Brookings Institution. Washington, D.C., 2003.

Süssmuth, Rita, and Werner Weidenfeld (eds.). *The European Union's Responsibilities Towards Immigrants*. Gütersloh, 2005.

Szabo, Stephen F. *Parting Ways: The Crisis in German-American Relations*. Washington, D.C., 2004.

Talbott, Strobe, and Nayan Chanda (eds.). *Das Zeitalter des Terrors. Amerika und die Welt nach dem 11. September*. Munich and Berlin, 2002.

Tewes, Henning. Das Zivilmachtkonzept in der Theorie der Internationalen Beziehungen. *Zeitschrift für Internationale Beziehungen* (4) 2: 347–359, 1997.

Thevessen, Elmar. *Die Bush-Bilanz. Wie der US-Präsident sein Land und die Welt betrogen hat*. Munich, 2004.

Todd, Emmanuel. *Weltmacht USA. Ein Nachruf*. Munich, 2003.

Transatlantic Strategy Group on Security and on Economics, Finance and Trade. *Transatlantic Responses to Global Challenges: The Way Forward, Discussion Outline and Follow-up Topics*. Bertelsmann Foundation, Center for Applied Policy Research. Gütersloh, 2003.

United States Government Printing Office. *Economic Report of the President. Transmitted to the Congress February 2003*. Washington, D.C., 2003.

Weidenfeld, Werner. Amerika bebt vor Zorn. *Süddeutsche Zeitung,* Oct. 9, 2002.

Weidenfeld, Werner (ed.). *Amsterdam in der Analyse.* Gütersloh, 1998.

Weidenfeld, Werner. Die Bilanz der Europäischen Integration 2002/2003. In *Jahrbuch der Europäischen Integration 2002/2003,* edited by Werner Weidenfeld and Wolfgang Wessels. Berlin, 2003a: 13–24.

Weidenfeld, Werner (ed.). *Die Europäische Verfassung in der Analyse.* Gütersloh, 2005a.

Weidenfeld, Werner (ed.). *Die Identität Europas. Fragen, Positionen, Perspektiven.* Munich, 1985.

Weidenfeld, Werner. Europa – aber wo liegt es? In *Europa-Handbuch,* edited by Werner Weidenfeld. Gütersloh, 2004a: 15–48.

Weidenfeld, Werner. Europäische Einigung im historischen Überblick. In *Europa von A bis Z. Taschenbuch der europäischen Integration,* edited by Werner Weidenfeld and Wolfgang Wessels. Munich, 2005b: 10–50.

Weidenfeld, Werner (ed.). *Europa Handbuch.* 2 vols., 3rd ed. Gütersloh, 2004b.

Weidenfeld, Werner. Europas Suche nach einer Identität. In *Europa von der Spaltung zur Einigung,* edited by Curt Gasteyger. Bonn, 1997a: 297–303.

Weidenfeld, Werner. Kühles Kalkül. Die neue Ära der transatlantischen Beziehungen. *Internationale Politik* (56) 6: 1–9, 2001.

Weidenfeld, Werner. *Kulturbruch mit Amerika? Das Ende transatlantischer Selbstverständlichkeit.* Gütersloh, 1997b. (English title *America and Europe: Is the Break Inevitable?* Gütersloh, 1997.)

Weidenfeld, Werner (ed.). *Maastricht in der Analyse.* Gütersloh, 1994.

Weidenfeld, Werner. Neue Ordnung, neue Mächte. *Welt am Sonntag,* Apr. 6, 2003b.

Weidenfeld, Werner (ed.). *Nizza in der Analyse. Strategien für Europa.* Gütersloh, 2001.

Weidenfeld, Werner, Caio Koch-Weser, C. Fred Bergsten, Walther Stützle and John Hamre (eds.). *From Alliance to Coalitions – The Future of Transatlantic Relations.* Gütersloh, 2004.

Weidenfeld, Werner, and Josef Janning. Europas Zukunftsfähigkeit – Herausforderungen, Grundlagen, Perspektiven. CAP Working Paper 12 2001. Centrum für angewandte Politikforschung. Munich, 2001.

Weidenfeld, Werner, and Wolfgang Wessels (eds.). *Europa von A bis Z. Taschenbuch zur europäischen Integration.* 8th ed. Bonn, 2002.

Weidenfeld, Werner, and Wolfgang Wessels (eds.). *Jahrbuch der Euro-päischen Integration 2003/2004.* Baden-Baden, 2004.

Wessels, Wolfgang. Die Europäische Union als Ordnungsfaktor. In *Die Neue Weltpolitik,* edited by Karl Kaiser and Hans-Peter Schwarz. Bonn, 1995.

The White House. Protecting our Nation's Environment. www. white house.gov/infocus/environment/index-cont.html (accessed January 13, 2005).

Wilson, Joseph C. *Politik der Wahrheit. Die Lügen, die Bush die Zukunft kosten könnten.* Frankfurt am Main, 2004.

Woodward, Bob.Plan of Attack. New York, 2004.

World Bank Group. *Global Monitoring Report.* 2004. 144.

World Tourism Organisation. World Tourism Barometer. June 2, 2004: 4.

World Trade Organisation (WTO). International Trade Statistics. Geneva, 2002. www.wto.org/english/res_e/statis_e/its2002_e/section1_e/i06. xls (accessed January 20, 2003).

World Trade Organisation. Ministerial Conference, Fourth Session, Doha, 9–14 November 2001: Ministerial Declaration, adopted on 14 November 2001. WTO Document WT/MIN(01)/DEC/1, November 20, 1001.

Zoellick, Robert. Unleashing the trade winds. *The Economist,* Dec. 7, 2002: 26.

The Author

Prof. Werner Weidenfeld, PhD
Member of the Executive Board,
Director of the Center for Applied Policy Research (CAP)

Werner Weidenfeld was born in 1947 and studied political science, history and philosophy at the University of Bonn. He wrote his doctoral thesis in 1971 on Gustav Stresemann's policy on England, completing post-doctoral work in 1975 in political science with a thesis on German European policy in the Adenauer era. He taught political science from 1975 to 1995 at the University of Mainz, while also teaching at the Sorbonne in Paris from 1986 to 1988. He served from 1987 to 1999 as coordinator of German-American Cooperation for the German government and received an honorary doctorate degree from the University of Middlebury (USA) in 1994. He has held the professorship for political systems and European unification at the University of Munich since 1995, and is the director of the Center for Applied Policy Research (CAP). He was a member of the board of trustees of the Bertelsmann Stiftung from 1990 to 2004; since 1992 he has been a member of the Bertelsmann Stiftung's executive board.